OFFBEAT
CAREERS

OFFBEAT CAREERS

THIRD EDITION

60 Ways To Avoid Becoming An Accountant

VIVIEN DONALD

KOGAN
PAGE

Acknowledgements

This book owes its existence to Al Sacharov whose Word of Mouth Press in Yonkers, New York, published *Offbeat Careers: 50 Ways to Avoid Being a Lawyer* in 1985.
The Foreword is taken from his book.

Cartoons by John Plum

First published in 1987
Second edition 1990
Third edition 1995, reprinted 1995

Kogan Page Limited
120 Pentonville Road
London N1 9JN
Text © Vivien Donald 1987, 1990, 1995.
Cartoons © Kogan Page Ltd 1987, 1990, 1995.

British Library Cataloguing in Publication Data

A CIP record for this book is available from the British Library.

ISBN 0-7494-1511-8

Typeset by DP Photosetting, Aylesbury, Bucks
Printed and bound in Great Britain by
Clays Ltd, St Ives plc

Contents

Foreword

Work does not have to be a four-letter word.

It can, in fact, be fun, challenging and a path for discovering the true spirit within each of us. With one-third of our time on earth spent working, it is important to make this time count. What then, constitutes good work? First, it should be harmonious with our personalities; second, it should earn enough to keep the wolf from the door; and third, it should be legal.

Within these parameters, there are hundreds of possibilities. The careers listed in this book are honest, challenging ways for men and women to live productive lives. They are offbeat in that they are jobs that have filtered through the cracks. They are not commonly mentioned in any career guide that is concerned with placing people in conventional positions. Their unique nature is in part due to the unique people who are needed to discover and pursue them.

As for the second part of the title, there are enough accountants who are overworked, unhappy and lonely. As one chartered accountant aptly stated, 'It is just not worth being miserable for the money.' Let's face it, a person's strong suit may not be a pinstripe. There are many people who could be a lot more fulfilled and happy if they did not feel compelled to follow some calling society deems prestigious.

So to everyone who is wrestling with the question, 'What do I want to be when I grow up,' I say let's show some imagination and daring.

Al Sacharov

Acupuncturi-t

CONTACT: The British Acupuncture Association,
34 Alderney Street, London SW1V 4EU;
0171 833 8164

EARNINGS: £25 per 45-minute session

SKILLS: Preferably medically based training and
qualifications; caring personality

The first acupuncturists were thought to have been soldiers of 7000 years ago in China, who wounded the opposition with arrows and were infuriated to note that instead of dropping down dead they became even healthier, recovering from their illnesses spontaneously and able to deal out free, remote control health treatment of their own.

After much experimenting with pointed wooden sticks and metal needles, the first equivalent to *The Lancet* was produced: a series of 34 books known as the *Nei Ching*, written between 2500 and 1000 BC, in which acupuncture was described as one aspect of the Chinese theory of holistic medicine.

Acupuncture recognises the Yin and Yang in the universe; opposing forces (such as hot and cold, masculine and feminine) that together influence the Ch'i, or life force. A person's Ch'i flows in the body along 26 meridians, each associated with one of the organs or body functions.

Ideally, acupuncturists should be in charge of their patients all the time, checking through pulse spots on the meridians the condition of the Yin and Yang flowing within the body. In this way they would be able to detect changes indicating illness before it becomes noticeable to the patient, and restore balance and harmony to the energy flow through the acupuncture points, keeping the patient healthy. In practice, of course, patients visit them when all else has failed, but over 70 per cent are reported to improve.

As well as using needles to stimulate the acupuncture

points, the acupuncturist may also use 'moxibustion' (small cones of burning herbs) and massage. Neither the needles nor the burning cause very much pain – the needles do not draw blood. Some acupuncturists use electrical stimulators instead of needles. Ear acupuncture, using points on the ear thought to relate to different parts of the body, is another offshoot.

A dramatic success story of acupuncture is its use in China as an anaesthetic during operations. In the West disorders treated include some respiratory conditions, gastro-intestinal disorders and various other problems including migraines and neuralgia. Acupuncture can also be successful in overcoming the withdrawal symptoms of people who give up smoking, alcohol or drugs.

Colleges that offer courses in acupuncture differ in their requirements; The British College of Acupuncture, 8 Hunter Street, London WC1N 1BN take only medically qualified students, including osteopaths, dentists, nurses, naturopaths and vets. The course lasts two to three years – students with skills in clinical diagnosis are exempted from the first year – and combines one weekend per month of training plus intensive home study and practical experience, leading to membership of the British Acupuncture Association; course fee for the first year is £1250.

Other colleges, such as the Chung San Acupuncture School (London) and the College of Traditional Acupuncture (Lea-mington Spa and Glasgow), take lay people as well as those with medical qualifications, but hold selection seminars to check suitability of applicants: that they have academic skills, are able to absorb information; that they have a caring attitude; that they are not school-leavers, but have some previous experience. Those accepted are of all ages and types, including pensioners. All courses are part time; costs can be around £2500 per year's course.

Ag-Pilot

CONTACT: Crop-spraying firms (in Yellow Pages)

SALARY: From £2000 per month, depending on experience;
            £30 to £50 per hour, freelance

SKILLS: Flying; commercial pilot's licence and 1000 flying
            hours

It is a dangerous way of life, flying at 100 feet above the ground and trying to keep within the perimeter of a field, while avoiding hazards that could be terminal, such as electricity pylons and trees; far removed from the auto-pilot boredom of a long-haul airline pilot's routine. Crop-spraying planes are specially designed and built and very strong, so a lucky pilot can walk away from a write-off crash.

There may be other types of difficult terrain to contend with in countries overseas, such as a 2000 ft canyon in Oman; for ag-pilots work all over the world, chasing the seasons. In the UK the season is June, July and part of August, with some top dressing of fertiliser work in February, March and April; then a pilot might be off to South Africa, Sudan, the Middle East, Egypt or Papua New Guinea for cotton and fruit crop spraying before snatching a holiday and returning to the UK.

Many of the pilots are New Zealanders and Australians, who have grown up with crop spraying at home and are highly skilled, used to coping with the different conditions in other countries. Others on the circuit, charging very competitive rates, are pilots from Poland and Ethiopia – who tend to fly a little too wildly.

Helicopters are taking over from fixed-wing aircraft, because they are safer and can turn within the perimeter of a field, or at the edge of woods or jungle, whereas a fixed-wing aircraft has to take up extra space for turning, coming closer to villages and outlying houses. Planes fly every day except when there is rain or winds over 10 knots.

Crop-spraying pilots (ag-pilots is their own term; 'cowboy'

is definitely unacceptable) work freelance, but do not own their aircraft, which belong to the crop-spraying companies. There are several companies in the UK, operating, of course, in the arable farming areas of the country, and also in non-arable areas of Scotland, Ireland and Wales, where they're deployed in forestry and on bracken spraying.

Companies may be willing to sponsor a pilot on an 'ag-aviation' course, to learn about the skills of low-level flying, how to operate the spraying gear and mix the chemicals used, as well as learning about the chemicals themselves. New chemicals have been developed that are environment friendly.

Before applying to a crop-spraying company, it is necessary to have a commercial pilot's licence (helicopter or fixed-wing) plus 1000 hours' flying experience. This is normally needed for insurance purposes and is usually made up with work such as air-taxiing or pleasure-flying at the seaside. The courses in agricultural aviation include some hours of flying as well. Silsoe College, Cranfield University, Bedfordshire, has an annual two-week course; some pilots do courses in California or Florida, where they may be found work to boost their flying hours, then it is back to the UK or off across the fields of the world.

Astrologer

CONTACT: The Astrological Association, 396 Caledonian Road, London N1 1DN; 0171 700 3746

EARNINGS: From £45 per consultation

SKILLS: No special skills; interest in people; confidence in yourself

'It's all in the stars' is the keynote of astrology – not only for those seeking signs of love and romance in the stars column of their newspaper, but for sober businesspeople, too. Even psychologists Jung and Eysenck became converted to astrology, and in France a mathematician, Michel Gauguelin, has carried out a survey that reveals a significant relationship between certain astrological signs and the professions of people whose time of birth as well as date were accurately known.

In Britain, where the time of birth is not automatically recorded, there is more difficulty in getting hold of all the facts the astrologer needs. Charts are worked out on the basis of the day, month, year, local time and place of birth; without accurate information it is impossible to give a complete analysis, but normally enough is provided to help the astrologer.

Subjects covered include character analysis, future trends, business advice, relationships, world affairs, medical astrology and advice on the very best time on the best day for important events such as getting married or signing documents.

Astrologers work either by direct consultation or by written or cassette-recorded reports, though personal consultations are normally thought best, so that the client's circumstances and background can be taken into account when the chart is being discussed.

A consultation may involve an hour or longer in preparation beforehand on an analysis of the client's chart from birth details taken when the appointment is made; then the consultation may take around one and a half hours and the client is given a taped or typed report with their chart and important dates for the year ahead. A report on tape is useful as the client can play it back any time, maybe in the car, and get a boost from listening to the astrologer's voice – many people go to an astrologer for help when they feel their lives are in a mess (and for career guidance, too).

Astrologers normally start by giving consultation to friends; then eventually someone phones and says: 'You don't know me, but ...' – and that is when they begin charging! Getting clients by recommendation is less risky than by advertising, as people who've made an appointment through an ad may not turn up. A good astrologer can be very busy. An average fee for a consultation in London is £65, rising to £100 or more for a very good astrologer. Outside London, charges are normally lower – check by finding out what the rate is in the area.

As astrologers work from home, it's a career that is popular with young mothers and retired people – but they do need qualifications.

Courses run by the colleges include correspondence courses, evening and day classes (some run by local authorities), seminars and summer schools. Certificate and Intermediate courses are designed for beginners; Diploma courses are for advanced students who want to become fully qualified astrologers. The Diplomas are internationally recognised as professional qualifications and a high standard of knowledge and practical application is expected. Once qualified, astrologers are listed, together with details of the areas of astrology in which they specialise.

Auctioneer

CONTACT: ISVA (Incorporated Society of Valuers and Auctioneers), 3 Cadogan Gate, London SW1X 0AS; 0171 235 2282

EARNINGS: Starting salary as trainees, £8000 to £10,000; fully qualified self-employed in partnerships with high earnings, especially in London

SKILLS: Academic abilities plus quick thinking, selling skills and talent for stimulating enthusiasm in an audience; loud voice

Like an actor, an auctioneer works to an audience, trying to inspire a responsive feedback from the buyers sitting on Lot 107 (Victorian mahogany dining chair and an oak ditto on turned baluster legs with under-stretchers) and encouraging them to get carried away and bid vast sums for Lot 86 (grey-painted heavy vice and set of drain rods).

Not all auctions are at the multi-million pound art market level, as seen on television, and not all involve antiques. It is part of the auctioneer's skill (and training) to be able to conduct auctions in livestock, scrap metal, commercial or residential property, old farm machinery, industrial machinery, fruit trees for orchards, bulbs (for planting), surplus government stock (could be Second World War gas masks), or the contents of country houses, with furniture and fine art.

Some of these sales take place away from the auction rooms, on site or in markets. An auctioneer who may have been selling vintage cars one week could be assessing the qualities of a top-class breeding ram as it enters the ring the following week. The most riotous auction of the year can be the Christmas Eve turkey sale – when guilt-ridden husbands stagger from their office parties remembering that they promised to take home the Christmas lunch.

The ability to think on your feet is an essential asset when conducting an auction; a reserve price may have been agreed with the client on an item, reserve bids may have been left by absent buyers, the porters may also have been asked to bid and all of these figures and possibilities, plus the proper worth of the item, must be in the auctioneer's mind as the bids mount up – some, it is sometimes suggested, taken 'off the wall' from an imaginary bidder in an attempt to push up the price. It would be no good ending up with a bid off the wall, though, if no member of the audience topped it. The skill involves thinking fast, having a feel for the audience, noting who is likely to bid, adapting to changing situations and keeping the pace lively.

Although the auctioneers of the prestigious auction houses of London and New York may be experts in their subjects, such as fine china or silver, most will have built up their knowledge of a wide range of subjects with experience based on training, so that they are able to advise their clients as to the value of goods, and compile the sale catalogues.

It is possible to join a firm as a porter or YT trainee and learn enough eventually to conduct auctions. A degree in history of art may be an advantage for those applying to a fine-art auction house, but selling skills are more important, especially in the busy residential property sector. Many auctioneers are professionally trained as surveyors or valuers and are partners in their own firms, belonging to the Royal Institution of Chartered Surveyors (RICS), 12 Great George Street, London SW1P 3AD or to the ISVA, the professional Society of Valuers and Auctioneers (address above).

Ballet Shoe Maker

CONTACT: Freed of London, 62–64 Well Street, Hackney,
            London E9 7PX; Gamba; Anello and Davide

EARNINGS: £250 to £350 per week, on piece work

SKILLS: Manual dexterity; attention to detail

A young dancer, pirouetting on one foot, puts the equivalent of 2½ tons in weight on to her point and the pleated satin tip of her shoe. No wonder she needs a steady supply of new shoes if she is not to come off stage with holes in her toes. The New York City Ballet is able to afford two new pairs for their dancers during prestige performances, and hundreds of new shoes every year for each girl. Our companies cannot be so spendthrift, but even so, they will take as many as 30 pairs per girl on a four-week foreign tour.

Each of the ballet shoes is handmade on an individual last, and the ballerina is so sensitive about her feet that she will try all the ballet shoe makers in a factory until she finds one making a shoe that exactly suits her and stick with him like glue until one or other of them retires. A dancer's feet are constantly changing; her roles and techniques, too; so there are always adjustments to be made.

Very important is the moulding of the block of a point shoe. It is made of a mixture of paper and hessian and paste, which starts as a soft and jellylike material and by the time it has been beaten into shape has become as firmly set as papier mâché, moulded to the dancer's shape.

The shoes are made following a very old method, now unique in the shoe trade: the inside-out method. Shoes vary in length and construction of the block, in the type of insole used and up to ten different measurements round the shoe – all must be exact. The maker lasts the shoe up, then forms the shoe inside out and sends it off to a machinist to be stitched, before finishing off his work on it. The top line is cut into shape and bound by someone else. No two makers will make exactly the same shoe, even using the same last. Wages are paid by piece work; in the top range a maker can turn out 42 pairs of shoes per day; others may settle for only 24 pairs.

Point shoes are made with cotton-lined satin, but practice and male dancers' shoes are of very soft leather or canvas. The function of a man's shoe is to protect the foot and support it enough to help him gain extra strength for the push off into a flying leap. He needs extra strength for holding the ballerinas aloft, too; the girls' shoe sizes have become larger over the years as ballerinas have become taller. American dancers in particular are tall and athletic; perhaps they will soon start lifting the men.

Ballet shoe-making firms may also supply shoes to ballet companies abroad in Japan, New Zealand, Australia and Europe; but not in Russia and other East European countries, where the theatre is a complex comprising all forms of entertainment, including the circus, drama and ballet, and where the workshops build scenery and make costumes as well as shoes.

In this country the factories make all types of theatrical and dance shoes, including the special designs for ballroom, jazz and tap dancing, and anything from a Roman sandal to a twenty-first century space boot for the theatre. Theatrical shoe craftsmen are expected to have some shoemaking experience, but the ballet shoe makers are trained from scratch. Staff stay with a factory for a long time, so the turnover is low and openings are few. The job does not, unfortunately, bring a steady supply of free tickets to the ballet, but it does give a chance of working with the world's top ballerinas.

Band Roadie

CONTACT: Local pop groups appearing in your area

EARNINGS: From nil to £50 per day basic up to £450 to £700 per week for a freelance worker; £200 per week when retained by a band, rising to £600 when the band is on tour (plus £30 daily living expenses in Europe, $50 in the USA)

SKILLS: Roadies need to be fit, prepared to be away from home on tours for long periods, have a basic working knowledge of electronics, and be able to co-exist with a roadie team on the road. A driving licence is useful but not essential

While the ideal pop star has a charismatic stage presence, the ideal roadie is one who is never seen. Stage absence means he has done his groundwork properly, though he may stand fretting out of sight during a concert in case anything goes wrong with the equipment. When everything is set up and ready to go, and there are 50,000 or so people in the audience, there can be 'quite a buzz' when the band hits the stage – and everything works right.

Roadies begin by helping out friends who belong to a pop group, loading their amplifier, drums and so forth into the hired van, and setting it all up on stage for local gigs. That will give them the experience that they'll be asked about when they go for interviews. The next stage is working in a loading crew (not a road crew), working locally, doing the donkey work and making maybe £50 per day. Skills in handling the equipment are picked up along the way.

Some roadies specialise in guitars and amps, others in drums or synthesizers. Others still specialise in lighting, sound or 'rigging' (hanging equipment from the roof), as stage managers or as floor managers, though when the chips are down and there is a panic on, everyone will do what has to be done. Bands are varied in the equipment that they use. Some need roadies for recording and rehearsal times; others only during a tour. When the band is on the road there may be a travelling crew of 14: four to deal with lighting, four sound people to set up the 'black boxes', one rigger, two in charge of the van gear, stage manager and two caterers. They live in the sleeper bus, but not much; hours can run from 7 am to 2 am. Living on a bus with 13 other people for a month is like living in a (comfortable) submarine, so any arguments have to be sorted out speedily.

A major tour with a big name like the Rolling Stones or Michael Jackson can mean 60 to 70 large, 38-ton trucks, and around 200 to 300 people – with caterers for the catering staff! First out of bed in the morning, and last to bed at night, the catering staff are at the bottom of a hierarchy that starts with the tour manager (who can be earning over £2500 a week plus first-class expenses with a big name) and continues down through the production manager, stage manager, backline technicians (instrument tuners), sound technicians, lighting technicians, riggers, scaffolders and truck drivers.

Those who are lucky, are good workers and understand the equipment can eventually work for 52 weeks of the year, though they need perseverance and must be prepared to spend time sitting around twiddling their thumbs waiting for the next job. On the road, money earned depends on the success of the band. A big American band in America may be able to pay $1000 a week (£620), but a British band on the same circuit may be able to pay only half that amount, so roadies doing the same job but with different bands may be getting twice as much – or half as much. It's up to the employer to decide whether you are worth the money you are asking!

It's a high-pressure world, complex and unique, but away from the 9 to 5 routine, which is why people like it. You can find yourself in some very strange and exotic places in the world, with the bands travelling not just to America and Europe, but around the globe to Australia, Japan, China and, increasingly, India.

Beautician

CONTACT: British Association of Beauty Therapy and Cosmetology Ltd, Parabola House, Parabola Road, Cheltenham, Gloucestershire GL50 3AH; 01242 570284

EARNINGS: From £6000 per annum, plus commission; beauty therapist £8000 per annum, plus commission

SKILLS: Sound educational background – studies in anatomy and physiology are an advantage; pleasant personality, enthusiasm and ability to deal tactfully and sympathetically with people

Everyone wants to look beautiful, as the make-up counters prove; not even men are exempt nowadays, especially those involved in the entertainment business. So there are jobs for

experienced beauty experts in films and television, as well as in the beauty salons and cosmetic houses.

A beautician, not quite the same as a beauty therapist, specialises in skin care, facial treatments, make-up, manicuring, pedicuring and removing unwanted hair using wax. She (hes are very rare) will also tint eyelashes and eyebrows, and apply eyelash extensions. A beauty therapist is concerned with shape: with body treatments that help clients to slim and tone up their muscles, losing both weight and inches, and to relax. Someone who has combined both types of training can qualify as an aestheticienne and, of course, improve their chances of an interesting job in a salon, health farm or club, on board a luxury liner or with the stars of the entertainment world (including politicians doing the party political broadcast TV spot).

Courses are run in colleges of technology and other further education colleges, private schools and sometimes in salons. A beautician course lasts from six months to a year. The course for an assistant beautician, designed mainly for people already working in hairdressing, is shorter. The syllabus for a full course includes skin care, electrical facial treatments, make-up, pedicure, manicure, face, neck and shoulder massage, waxing, depilation, cosmetic science, first aid, salon procedure, hygiene, ethics and business organisation – useful for those intending to set up their own salon or work freelance, visiting clients in their own homes.

The length of the course for those studying for NVQ/SVQs depends on how quickly a trainee can gain them in individual units or a number of units; NVQ/SVQs can be taken up to Level 3. There are international examinations for certificates and diplomas for which candidates must study for a minimum number of hours, depending on the final qualification. Those studying for an Assistant Beautician Certificate must complete 125 hours; and those studying for a Beautician Diploma must complete 300 hours.

Fees for training depend on the centre providing the programme, and on how long it takes. Grants are not normally available, but the Confederation of International Beauty Therapy and Cosmetology suggests contacting your local education authority.

Blast Cleaner

CONTACT: Stone Federation, 82 New Cavendish Street, London W1M 8AD; 0171 580 5404

EARNINGS: From £180 to £250 per week; hourly rates would be £4 to £6 – the higher rate for those who can do metal spraying and paint spraying, and fix their own gun.

SKILLS: Physical fitness; for some work, no fear of heights

Blast cleaners dress up like spacemen to strip years of grime and pollution, rust and paint off buildings and monuments, bridges and ships and the interiors of old houses. They may work for a large blast-cleaning company, such as those cleaning city-centre buildings who run their own training programmes, or on a self-employed basis, specialising in a particular type of cleaning.

The space suit is to protect them against the dust created by blast cleaning, so that they can breathe their own clean air supply. There may even be an intercom system installed as well. The cleaning is done by bombarding the surface with abrasives, using a powerful air compressor, blasting pot (to hold the abrasives) and hose. The abrasives vary according to the surface material and range from crushed egg shells for delicate wood to glass beads and grit. Black walnut shells, crushed fruit pips and ground rice hulls have been used in the aircraft industry to clean carbon deposits from engine pistons and specially manufactured abrasives include steel wire, nail 'whiskers' and brass or copper shot. Dust is kept down by combining water with the abrasive.

Since the Clean Air Act, it has been worthwhile cleaning up the encrustations or pollution on city buildings. Even Nelson on his column is not too grand for a wash and brush-up, lofty though he is. For some buildings, cleaning is done by combining water with acid; occasionally water may be used on its own.

Working for one of the large blast-cleaning companies could mean perching on scaffolding round a cathedral, grand Victorian town hall or large country mansion. Other projects could be bridges such as the Severn Bridge or the Clifton Suspension Bridge, which must have rust corrosion removed regularly. It is not only large structures that need cleaning and restoration: steam railway engines, vintage car coach work and the woodwork of the old sailing ships, such as Captain Scott's *Discovery* and HMS *Victory*, have been stripped using blast machines.

Small businesses can be busy doing interior restoration on houses, stripping paint and varnishes from woodwork to reveal the original. Blast cleaning, though very dusty, is less of a fire risk than stripping by using a blow torch on old wood, and faster than chemical stripping. There is an interest now in removing the black staining on beams in period houses and burnishing the wood with wax.

Setting up as a blast cleaner would cost around £2000 for machinery and protective clothing, plus hire of compressor, and a van. Training in use of the equipment is given by manufacturers, such as Hodge Clemco Ltd, Orgreave Drive, Handsworth, Sheffield S13 9NR.

Bodyguard/ Security Guard

CONTACT: Security firms; International Professional Security Association (IPSA), IPSA House, 3 Dendy Road, Paignton, Devon TQ4 5DB; 01803 554849

EARNINGS: £60 to £200 per day; £120 to £130 average (bodyguard); £2 to £6 per hour (security guard)

SKILLS: Age 18 to 55. Able to think on your feet, adapt and improvise, to work on your own or as part of a group; not panic under pressure; interpersonal skills; integrity

A bodyguard is hired to protect an individual person (and sometimes his or her family as well) from the risk of kidnapping as well as violence or terrorism; a security guard protects property. If you watch the news on television, you'll be able to pick out the bodyguards surrounding rock and pop stars, sports personalities, politicians, heads of industry and other rich and famous business people, scientists and other high-threat people while they are out and about in public life. In the US they'll be carrying guns, but in this country civilian bodyguards are not allowed the use of firearms.

Before the cameras arrive at an event an advance party of bodyguards will have checked the venue, looking in the rubbish bins, and at surrounding buildings. The tramp in the doorway could be in counter-surveillance – looking to see who's looking around. There may be several people in the personal escort team with the VIP, or the bodyguard may be the driver. If the VIP goes abroad, the bodyguard goes along as well, and can spend a lot of time out of the country. At home there will perhaps be another close protection team of 'residence' bodyguards looking after the family. A bodyguard, who works on a 12-hour basis, becomes a confidant, looking after the subject's well-being as well as his or her physical security.

Bodyguard/Security Guard

Bodyguards are often recruited from ex-Servicemen, ex-doormen, or martial arts practitioners. Extel Security does nine-day courses for bodyguards, starting with a two-day weekend course at £100 and, for those considered suitable, a follow-up five-day course at £650.

A security guard will be given training by the company lasting about six weeks, followed by on-the-job training which continues on a regular basis. There will also be tests, including psychometric testing, as part of the recruitment procedure.

A company such as Securicor protects both sites and goods in transit. The goods may be cash being delivered to banks, or collected from shops, or credit cards or other valuables. Security firms are also hired by organisations such as local authorities to collect council house rents.

On-site guarding covers mainly business premises, which are often secured by a fence and gatehouse. The guards staff the gatehouse and reception to check on arrivals, and patrol the whole area, keeping an extra eye out for unusual activity through CCTV (closed-circuit television). In office buildings, guards are on duty at night to patrol the empty offices.

Security guards always work with the back-up of another guard, or the company's main control room.

As well as being trained in patrolling and searching, some aspects of the law, and firefighting, some security guards are trained in dog handling and self-defence, and how to conduct body searches and bomb detection work if the company has been hired to work in specialist areas such as airports and conferences. There are already NVQ/SVQs at Level 2 for security guards, with new qualifications in aviation security, transporting property under guard, specification, installation and maintenance of security systems.

Induction, career foundation, supervisory and managing security courses are organised by IPSA, which has a correspondence college leading to City & Guilds qualifications.

You may not always be able to identify bodyguards, but you can find yourself tripping over uniformed security guards everywhere: strolling through shopping arcades, blocking the pavement outside the banks and checking your hand luggage at the airport. Many of the jobs once done by the police are now handled by contract security firms in what has become an expanding industry.

Bow Maker

CONTACT: College addresses given below and individual bow makers

EARNINGS: Depend on speed, experience and quality of work; top-quality bows sell for £600 up to £2000

SKILLS: Manual dexterity

Making bows for stringed instruments is a different craft from the making of the instruments themselves, although college courses combine the two skills. Bow makers work with exotic woods such as South American snakewood, pernambuco (once used as a purple dye, so sweaty hands cause problems) and ebony. The woods may be intricately carved with fluting or reeding, and the 'frogs' that hold the horsehair as well as the screw buttons and slides that control its tension may be made of imitation ivory or tortoiseshell

embellished with mother of pearl, gold or silver. There is plenty of scope for artistic talent.

Bows are made not only for violins, but violas, cellos, double basses, bass violas, and viols as well. They may be modern designs, or copies of beautiful old renaissance and baroque models. A bow takes at least a week to make, if it is of good quality.

Colleges that include bow making in their courses for musical instrument making are the London Guildhall University; Newark and Sherwood College, Friary Road, Newark, Nottinghamshire NG24 1PB; City of Leeds College of Music, Cookridge Street, Leeds LS2 8BH. The London Guildhall University requires four GCE O level/GCSE passes for its two-year full-time course.

A more comprehensive training in bow making is given by apprenticeship to a bow-making firm. Most bow makers are self-employed and, although they are very busy, there are not many who are prepared to take on an apprentice or assistant. However, some are prepared to give training to school leavers. Bow makers advertise in *Strad* magazine, available from music shops or through newsagents.

Good bow makers not only supply bows to the great soloists and orchestras all over the world, but can themselves go anywhere in the world to work if they have the right training and qualifications (Europe is inclined to frown on those who do not have good qualifications). However, there are many bow makers working on their own who have learned the special skills involved after training in other crafts.

A large part of the work of the various firms that supply bows is in their repair and maintenance. Many of the people working for them may never make a complete bow, but only parts of bows, or be involved exclusively in repair work.

Cartoonist

CONTACT: Editors of magazines and newspapers

EARNINGS: From £250 per day, if successful

SKILLS: Artistic ability, especially for comic strips;
humorous view of topical events

Cartoons have changed since the 1860s, when George du Maurier was drawing them for *Punch* – beautifully detailed illustrations, comments on social life that no longer seem particularly funny. Now the style of drawing is much simpler, reduced almost to symbolism in some cases, with more political bite. The other types of cartoons are the regular comic strips in newspapers and magazines and specially compiled books, and drawings illustrating a book's content, as in this one.

Cartoonists may have to think up their own wording, or be given all of it by an editor; or the final result may be a mixture of ideas from editor and artist. On a newspaper, the political cartoonist is a member of the staff, and is given an idea to work on, making a certain political point, by two or three editors and sub-editors. The cartoonist scribbles roughly on a blackboard set up in the office or studio, aided and abetted or criticised by the editors and sub-editors until the theme is thrashed out and approved, and the final drawing can be made. If the editor of the paper has a 'down' on a certain politician, he may get the cartoonist in and ask him to work on a remark the unfortunate MP has made in Parliament or on television the night before. Cartoonists are not always able to work freely with their own brand of political satire as they did in the days of David Low.

Other cartoons are done on a freelance basis. The hopeful cartoonist does the drawing, writes the caption and sends it off, nicely packed, to an editor – who probably sends it back because, unless it is brilliant, work from an unknown artist will not be used. Persistence with well-drawn, good ideas can pay off, though, especially if the gag is topical, and once the editor has bought one cartoon, then further acceptance on that publication is much more likely. The rate for a single cartoon varies from £25 to £50 up to £1000 for a 'star', with around £75 as an average. But a beginner may get only £15 – one experienced cartoonist reckons it takes about five years to get established.

Book illustration involves a certain amount of research, so that the drawing is a reasonably accurate representation. Very often children's book illustration is done by women, whose approach to the subject can be more sympathetic.

Comic strips cover all sorts of subjects: Andy Capp-type humour, space adventure, animal characterisations. They may be complete in themselves, with three or four panels, or a continuous story unfolding daily, in a newspaper, or four or five pages in a comic book with the story continuing in the next issue.

There is a big demand for good artists for the comic strip type of work. Most of the artists will have had an art school training, but will have developed a kind of shorthand of fast drawing, using their own style and tricks. The rate per page of comic strip work could be £250 to £450 for script and artwork, with 60 per cent going to the artist and 40 per cent going to the script writer (who can work faster). Some artists may do one page in a day, some two pages, and a very experienced and fast artist can do three pages in a day. A cartoon strip, with artist writing his own captions, may earn £300 to £700 per week; this could be doubled or trebled by fees for syndication if the strip sells well worldwide. Cartoonists can make a very good living – as much as £70,000 per year; and £150,000 pa is a possibility.

For a leaflet entitled *Getting Started in Comics*, contact the Comics Creators Guild, c/o The London Sketch Club, 7 Dilke Street, London SW3 4JE; 0171 352 8209.

One thing you do need is self-discipline: the ability to sit at the drawing board at home and work through for a set number of hours every day – and see the funny side of life.

Casting Director

CONTACT: Producers' Alliance for Film and Television (PACT),
            Gordon House, Greencoat Street, London SW1P 1PH

EARNINGS: Average, £35,000 per annum

SKILLS: Very good memory; organised; able to make quick
            calculations; good with people

It may surprise those who have the old image of the casting director's couch in mind to know that most casting directors in this country are women; it is one of the few highly paid jobs that it is easy for a woman to get into, even through secretarial work, because there is no male-dominated cartel.

Casting directors are freelances, commissioned by directors or producers. Some work on films for cinema, or for television productions, or specialise in commercials, but as there are not that many entirely British films, casting directors tend to be involved in both films and television productions, especially now that there are more television film-type productions, made on film rather than in the studio on video.

Each production is dealt with by one casting director working alone. She is given the script to read, then does a breakdown of characters and makes suggestions of actors and actresses for all the characters. She must phone their agents to check whether they are available, and is also responsible for negotiating the fee, on behalf of the film's director (with the exception of BBC productions). The final decision for casting rests with the director; the casting director's job is to suggest names, and chivvy up a decision as the deadline nears.

A lot of time is spent in the theatre or cinema, assessing the performances and capabilities of actors and actresses. When casting for a project it is important to get both the balance and the chemistry between performers right - it might, for instance, involve choosing people to play the members of a family. There can be risks if an actor proves not to be capable of a difficult part when the cameras are on him - or an actress is found to have taken to hitting the bottle.

The time taken depends on the length of a project and its complexity; 12 hours of television may take six months to cast. A job like *Jewel in the Crown* could involve going to India to cast all the smaller parts, but that sort of chance does not come up very often. Generally, a project takes six to eight weeks, with variable salaries - around £500 per week if working for the BBC, £800 per week working for an independent company, and more, £1200 to £1500, for television commercials, which is less enjoyable work; £1200 for a (cinema) feature film. It is possible to earn £75,000 pa - but out of that you would have to pay assistants. Some weeks, of course, you could be earning nothing at all, as it is freelance work.

Some people go into the work as secretaries and assistants to freelance casting directors, or through working for a television company, or with a drama school background. It is advisable to become a member of BECTU (Broadcasting Entertainment Cinematograph and Theatre Union). Normally you must work for two years as assistant to a casting director before getting an assistant casting director's ticket, then work for a further two years in the same job before being a fully fledged member, and able to work on your own. There is an enormous amount of knowledge of the acting profession to be absorbed at the beginning, although eventually it is just a question of getting to know the new members that arrive each year. A play with an unusual background, such as one about Asians, would mean finding out all about a different group of actors.

It is important to get on with people well to get things done. Having a head for figures is useful, too: sometimes you may be asked to budget a project, or get involved with selling network or syndicated showings of the actors' work in America. A big plus of the work is that production directors and producers are usually very pleasant to work with.

Chicken Sexer

CONTACT: Association of British Chick Sexers, 54 Mercia Avenue, Charlton, Nr Andover, Hampshire SP10 4EJ

EARNINGS: From £12,500 per annum; £20 to £30 per hour freelance

SKILLS: Good eyesight; manual dexterity; ability to get up early in the morning, work in chick dust in 80°F (24°C) temperatures

Another skill imported from the mysterious Orient, chicken sexing was first (and is still) carried out in this country by Japanese and South Koreans who had discovered how to save two months' feeding costs on unwanted (male) chicks by identifying their sex at hatching, instead of later.

There are three methods: sex-linked and feather-sexing are normally done by staff in the hatcheries. Feather-sexing is done by looking at the positioning of the flight feathers; sex-linked chicks are sexed by colour – brown chicks are pullets and white ones are cocks.

Vent-sexing is highly skilled, and is a tricky and delicate operation (very indelicate for the chick). It involves opening up the vent and judging by the formation of the skin, texture and colour on an area of 1mm or less in size, whether the chick is male or female. Vent-sexing is used for breeding stock.

Not only is good eyesight needed, but also calm and gentle handling to avoid rupturing the skin. A skilled vent-sexer can deal with 500 to 1000 chicks in an hour at about £2 per hundred – there are only about 50 people of this standard in the country. Feather-sexing is around 3300 per hour, at 50p per hundred.

Hatcheries start work at 5am to 6am, so the chicken sexer often has to be up well before the lark. Freelance workers are employed through agencies, so may have long journeys to the hatcheries, or may spend a week away from home; expenses

GIRLS   BOYS   DON'T KNOWS

are not normally paid. A day's work consists of three to five hours of very fast work, about four days a week.

With feather-sexing, undertaken by hatchery staff, on the increase there is less work for vent-sexers at the moment, except with the large breeders who raise the stock from which the meat and egg-laying birds will be produced, and with those who have specialist breeds.

Training, given by the agencies, can take up to two years, though someone who turns out to have a 'natural' skill could be working alone within six to nine months. The training could involve practising on altogether half a million day-old cockerels at a hatchery, is 'hell' and only one in ten complete training – so it can be an expensive undertaking for an agency.

Vent-sexers may also work on ducks, turkeys and game birds and can find their services in demand on the continent as well as at home.

Chimney Sweep

CONTACT: National Association of Chimney Sweeps, St Mary's Chambers, 19 Station Road, Stone, Staffordshire ST15 8JP

EARNINGS: From £10,000 per annum; turnover around £24,000

SKILL: Meeting people

If you look right up inside a Georgian chimney, you might see the jutting bricks, set one above the other, that the little chimney boys once used to help them 'walk' up inside, bracing their backs against the opposite wall as they struggled sootily upwards. And if you go outside and look up at the chimney stacks, you'll see that they are sited far away from the fireplaces, so that the chimneys must wind in all directions to avoid the intervening rooms and finally reach the stacks and open air.

Today's chimney sweeps don't have to climb, but they do still have to cope with the windings, and it's only experience that tells them by the messages fed back by the brush, what is happening up there. Architects such as Lutyens, priding themselves on a balanced effect, did not bother about the convolutions suffered by the chimney sweep's brushes to reach the strategically placed stacks. Chimneys can be 90 to 100 feet high.

In some places sweeps deal with nothing but bungalows – short and sweet. In industrial and commercial districts, the challenges are different again. Fuels used produce different deposits: soft or hard woods, coal, smokeless fuel, wood-burning stoves, oil boilers, gas flues. Insurance companies now demand that gas appliances are cleaned out regularly; in contrast to the wide old chimneys, their flues are only 4 inches across.

To set yourself up with all the different brushes and rods of the sweeping equipment and vacuum cleaner costs £2000–£3000 with really comprehensive set-ups costing still more, plus van, signwriting, insurance and advertising costs. Yellow Pages ads don't bring instant results, especially if there are several other sweeps in competition; watch out for closing dates, to avoid missing out for the first year. The work is seasonal; perhaps only two or three days' work per week for a quarter of the year, and there is wear and tear on equipment to consider.

Many sweeps combine the trade with a full-time job, as fireman, policeman, window cleaner, even college lecturer (mornings only). With the popularity of other modern heating systems like imitation gas log fires, there are not too many customers around, and the sweep has to charm those he does find so that they will ask him again. They may be nervous and apprehensive about a sweep coming into their homes (in Georgian times all sweeps were not only sooty, but also ex-convicts, and for some people the folk memory lingers on); so meeting people and putting them at their ease is all part of the job.

The National Association of Chimney Sweeps can offer training, and this is well advised, as an untrained sweep can be a danger to the public and to himself. Charging around £25 to £35 per job depending on area, a sweep will not make a fortune but have 'a reasonable little business'.

Clown

CONTACT: Clowns International, Secretary:
David McIntyre, Flat 1, 35 Park Wood Road,
Boscombe, Bournemouth, Dorset BH5 2BS

EARNINGS: 'Very little' to around £400 per week

SKILLS: Creativity; physical fitness; magnetism

There's more to clowning, say the traditionalists, than putting on make-up and calling yourself a clown. There's juggling, balancing tricks, plate-spinning, fire-eating, acrobatics and magic, as well as the slapstick humour, the comedy cars, the trouser-dropping, the tripping up and falling over.

Skills are built up with many years of hard practice and

clowns have their own specialities; not every clown in bowler hat, baggy trousers and sparkly jacket can balance a towering pile of 600 cups. The talent for making children – of all ages – laugh comes from observing the everyday things in life that can be funny and slipping them into the clowning routine; creating a gale of laughter from some perfectly ordinary object or activity.

Clowns are not confined to the two-minute run-in of a circus performance; they are to be found at children's tea parties, galas, carnivals, charity events, festivals and advertising promotions. The traditional way into clowning comes from learning the art from one of the old hands, from watching performances and getting involved with circuses and entertainers.

Most circus clowns are members of clowning families and have learnt their art from watching their parents; they may also have joined one of the excellent grant-aided schools in Europe for extra training. In a travelling village circus a clown may earn £100 to £150 per week; better-known clowns can ask around £400 and very big names can receive up to £1000 for a week's booking for an act (with all the props) that will entertain the audience for five to six minutes at each performance.

Those who want to get in on the act but don't have a circus background are more likely to do the rounds of the festivals as street entertainers, though earnings are 'very little'. They can pick up a few tricks at circus training schools: the Circus Space, Coronet Street, Hackney, London N1 6HD (0171 613 4141) and Zippo's Academy of Circus Arts, 174 Stockbridge Road, Winchester, Hampshire SO22 6RW (01962 877600), which provide tuition on the road, living with the circus.

Clown noses, unicycles, make-up, animal modelling balloons, helpful books and videos are to be found at the Oddball Juggling Shop, 56 Islington Park Square, London N1 1PX. Their props for jugglers include spinning plates, rings and cigar boxes, and fire clubs, devil sticks and cotton reel-shaped diabolos; they also run a workshop for would-be jugglers.

Clowns International conventions and festivals are great chances to see acts from all over the world.

Coach Tour Courier

CONTACT: English Tourist Board, Thames Tower, Black's Road, Hammersmith, London W6 9EL; 0181 846 9000; or local regional tourist board

SALARY: £65.70 half day; £100 to £110 full day (London Blue Badge Guide, 1994/95 rates)

SKILLS: Articulate; good at communicating; ability to do research; enthusiasm; confidence; caring nature; foreign languages

The coach tour courier is the one that you see talking into a microphone to a row of interested (or not) faces peering through the tour-bus window. The aim of the talk is to bring the history and character of the area alive.

A courier, or tour manager, is the company's representative, particularly on holidays abroad, responsible mainly for looking after the tourists and either arranging guided tour programmes or perhaps showing the tourists round the sights personally. At home the coach company may expect the coach driver to do the running commentary, or use a self-trained courier to do the job, or take on a highly trained Blue Badge Guide.

Whoever does the job needs to be good at doing research to make a success of it. While a coach driver in an unfamiliar area may be able to make up for shortcomings in local knowledge by good-natured waffle and jokes, a driver or courier will make more at the end of the day (in tips) with a well-informed spiel.

Drivers and couriers working for coach companies can build up knowledge of their area through research in the local library and tourist office, and by keeping up with events in the local papers. They need to make the talk interesting, about local people as well as places. Coach tour passengers like plenty of anecdotes, gossip and stories about the area and its people, and what went on in the past.

For tourists who like a more in-depth commentary covering history, architecture and art, a coach company will take on a Blue Badge Guide. These take a training course and examination run by one of the regional tourist boards for registration as a guide. Blue Badge Tourist Board Registered Guides are assessed on in-depth local knowledge, national 'core' knowledge and in presentational skills.

Each board's examinations cover its own area of the country, and the courses normally take two years, running during the winter. The part-time courses are heavily academic, with an entry examination covering questions on geography, history, architecture, the arts, literature, current events and the local area. Applicants should be aged over 23; there can be as many as 800 applications for 35 places.

The course combines lectures and practical training (including a useful session on breath control and voice projection). The fee is around £1450. The two sessions can be combined in an intensive seven-month course.

Once qualified, Blue Badge Guides will join the group of guides contacted by the local tourist office, and may specialise in a particular interest such as archaeology, or art galleries; if they have one or more foreign language they will specialise in looking after tourists from that country, or they may specialise in taking specific groups of people, such as the disabled. Foreign languages especially in demand on the training programme are combinations of European languages, in particular Russian, plus Oriental languages, such as Japanese, Korean and Thai.

Guides are normally self-employed, offering a freelance service to tour and coach operators or small groups with a specialist interest; some may be hired on short-term or seasonal contracts. The list of registered guides is circulated to tour operators, and ground handlers (the companies who deal with tourists from abroad); and guides also get work through guide-booking agencies.

The work is seasonal, from April to September, although in some parts of the country, particularly London, the work continues, though at a less busy rate, all through the year.

Costumier

CONTACT: Film and theatre costumiers in Yellow Pages

SALARY: From £10,000 to £15,000 per annum

SKILLS: Artistic; creative, able to work under pressure; able
              to translate two-dimensional drawings into
              garments

Costumiers spend a lot of their time looking through their stores to see what they have in stock that is suitable for a production before they get a tailor or costume maker to make up something new. Nothing is ever thrown away!

Costumier companies such as Angels & Bermans in London hire out costumes, dealing mainly with film work, and also with television, theatre and photographic work – styling for magazines and advertising. There is much less work for theatre than for films, the reason being that once a theatrical production has been costumed, the production could run on for some time at the theatre, so nothing new will be needed.

The Royal Opera House has its own wardrobe department for the costuming of three companies: the Royal Ballet, the Royal Opera and the Birmingham Royal Ballet. Here the costume supervisor is responsible for buying materials and providing the costumes the designer wants, and the costumier is the person who makes them up.

BBC TV Centre also has a vast stock of clothes and accessories which have to be raided before a new garment can be made or hired. One of the most tricky aspects of the job is to keep within the allocated budget.

The costume designer is the person responsible for translating what the director or choreographer has in mind for a production. The process begins with meetings, reading the script, so that they can handle the work as a team. The designer has to interpret the mood, characterisation and dramatic content of the work and do the period research. Specialised historical research starts yesterday, since even last year's fashions for both men and women are different, let alone those of 20, 50 or 100 years ago. The designer also needs to be aware of the etiquette of the period and the personal details that make the whole effect authentic.

The designer then approaches the costumiers either in-house or at the hire company to work with a costumier who specialises in the type of garments needed. The costumier has to understand what the designer has in mind, and come up with the goods – or garments.

Costumiers become very knowledgeable about periods and styles, such as the 1920s or '30s, or military costume.

At BBC TV Centre hiring from outside is considered if there is nothing suitable in the stores, which hold everything from Egyptian sarongs to bodices. Or a costume maker may be asked to knock up something new; how elaborate the costume ends up depends on how much is allowed in the budget.

The costumier, who may also have a copy of the script, is based in the clothes store and will have a detailed knowledge of the costume of the period. It can be hard work with long hours, some of them spent filming on location and in studio rehearsals, and a great deal of time is given over to shopping for suitable fabrics and accessories – always a tiring business – budgeting and doing the bills.

It's not all historical stuff, though. Costumiers also specialise in outfits for TV light entertainment: variety shows and musical productions.

You don't need to be a wizard with the sewing machine to become a costumier, although a degree in theatre or fashion helps those who want to get into the BBC. Many who start in the BBC work up to becoming design assistants and can eventually be theatre designers. It is possible for those who have an aptitude for the job to make a career change to work in one of the theatrical costumiers without any theatrical or fashion qualifications.

Colleges that have relevant courses include the London College of Fashion, Wimbledon School of Art, Central St Martins College of Art and Design, Bournemouth and Poole College of Art and Design (Costumes for TV course), City of Liverpool Community College, Manchester College of Arts and Handsworth College, Birmingham.

Croupier

CONTACT: British Casino Association, 29 Castle Street, Reading, Berkshire RG1 7SL; 01734 589191

SALARY: £10,500 to £17,500, London rates

SKILLS: Attractive appearance; good with figures; nimble fingers; good colour vision; age must be at least 18 to 25

Whatever the time of day, and wherever the place, for the croupier at the gaming tables it is always night, with heavy drawn curtains and shaded lights. Night-time begins at 2 pm and lasts until 4 am in Britain; in other countries or on board ship, it may be until the last customers leave the tables.

British croupiers are much sought after in casinos overseas

because they are well trained and their Gaming Board Certificate shows that their background has been vetted by the government-run Board, and that they have no criminal convictions. No croupier is allowed to deal without a certificate.

There is a trend for training to be done at independent training schools, but many national casino operating companies, such as Grosvenor Clubs, still offer training.

London's Mayfair has some very rich and plush clubs, but others are scattered throughout the country in large towns and holiday resorts. Salaries are considerably less in the provinces. Casino trainees are recruited through the local papers or radio and selected (from perhaps 600 to 700 applicants in London) by interview. They are given a simple maths test and checked for colour blindness and manual dexterity (for handling the gaming chips). The first training session, during which trainees are paid, lasts for five weeks, with lectures on grooming, customer relations, security, body language (how to stand at table and smile all the time) and initiation into the complexities of just one game – either American roulette or blackjack.

Once the trainees have gained the appropriate certificate, they go off on to the casino floor to practise their new skills for six to nine months, before being taught a second game and eventually, after another six to nine months, a third. After 18 months to two years, a croupier is eligible to be promoted to inspector.

There is no obligation to stay with the casino after training and many dealers ('croupiers' is an old French word) do go abroad to see the world, enjoy the Bahamas or Sun City; girls often go on to cruise ships. On the ships the work is hard, in confined conditions and pay is not so good, but the dealer can rely on tips (not allowed in Britain).

Croupiers who stay can make the job their career, going on to become pit boss (controlling one area of the casino) and then into management. Many large companies have their own management training scheme, covering employment law, public relations etc. Eventually they can hit the jackpot, as directors.

Gambling among croupiers is not allowed; they work eight-hour shifts, with the pressure relieved by half-hour rest breaks after every hour on duty. Uniforms and meals are provided plus social activities and, with companies that have other entertainment interests, cut-price theatre tickets – no bad deal.

Dance and Mime Animateur

CONTACT: Community Dance and Mime Foundation, 13–15
             Belvoir Street, Leicester LE1 6SL; 0116 2755057

SALARY: £9500 (trainee) to £22,900

SKILLS: Experience of community dance; programming and
             promotion skills; communication skills; administra-
             tive expertise; current driving licence and your own
             car an advantage

The job of dance and mime animateur is relatively new – the first few entered stage right in 1976 and there are now animateurs working in community dance throughout the UK. They are not always called animateurs. Sometimes the job title may be community dance worker, dance development officer or dance adviser. But the idea is to get the local community animated – coming alive with dance of all kinds. And it seems to be working! There are lively dance centres heaving with dancers doing everything from contemporary dance to the hugely popular South Asian dancing, particularly in the north of England.

No two animateurs do exactly the same work, but their main role is that of taking dance to the public, mainly in primary and secondary schools and community centres. This could involve arranging for a company to perform a type of dance, advertising the performance in the press and on posters, and preparing the audience beforehand by explaining the techniques – or getting them physically involved.

Animateurs may be employed by the local authority or regional arts board, or independent arts organisations and theatre companies. Although they are given an office to work from, animateurs spend a lot of time travelling to the various dance venues and schools, and liaising with local organisations.

As part of their work animateurs may teach dancing or do choreography for youth groups and local productions, but their job is mainly involved with more down-to-earth administration and marketing, community liaison, finance and fundraising (sometimes raising the money for their own salaries!). They may also need to employ dance teachers, as well as arranging performances and workshops by professional dance companies. The animateur may set up a project, and then need to find other dancers to carry on with it.

Classical ballet has been knocked off its points in community dance by people keen to have a go at something a little different: for instance, jazz exercise, flamenco, tap, belly dancing, contemporary dance and the varying forms of classical Indian dance. It is all a lot more entertaining than aerobics. Animateurs arrange classes in everything from Khathak and tango to mime and movement, for all ages, from toddlers to over-50s, and all abilities.

Though mime is very often part of the job title, most animateurs work mostly with dance. Some animateurs specialise in mime, others specialise in working with a particular dance style or technique, or for a specific group within the community. Or they may specialise in management and administration as a coordinator or director.

Some animateurs work full time for regional arts boards (though most contracts are for one year only, or three years at most) or are attached to dance companies, their brief being to educate audiences and the public at large about the dancing. Most are self-employed freelances.

Although some of the first animateurs did not have full-time training as dancers, those employed now will have trained as dancers with one of the dance companies, or at the Laban Centre for Movement and Dance, and many have a teaching qualification. There is also an increasing number of relevant courses on dance in the community, such as the four-year BA Honours Dance in Society course at the University of Surrey. The Community Dance and Mime Foundation can confirm whether a course is suitable. Some Arts Council traineeship awards are given in dance administration.

Diver

CONTACT: For commercial diving: IMCA, The International
            Marine Contractors Association, 177A High Street,
            Beckenham, Kent BR3 1AH; 0181 663 3859
            For sports diving: British Sub-Aqua Club, Telfords
            Quay, Ellesmere Port, South Wirral, Cheshire
            L65 4FY; 0151 357 1951

SALARY: Commercial diving, around £35 to £80 per day to
            over £200 per day; sports diving, up to £25,000 per
            year

SKILLS: Age over 18; swimming; physical fitness; responsible
            attitude to safety

The two types of diving, commercial and sports, are very different. There is certainly much more glamour attached to sports diving, which involves, at the professional level, teaching people to dive all around the world. As a sport connected to the leisure industry, it is an expanding business, taking place in some of the most exotic places on the tourist map; Thailand, Belize, the Red Sea, Mexico and Southern America, the Caribbean and especially Australia.

Commercial diving is more likely to mean working in the cold and murky waters round North Sea oil and gas platforms. Many commercial divers are already qualified as welders, blasters or fitters, or hold an engineering degree or diploma. Some of their work takes place at 200 or even 300 metres, living for days in pressure chambers; other jobs may mean no more than being half-submerged.

All diving demands a thorough understanding of winds, tides and time allowance, but diving in this environment is especially hazardous. The water may be so dark and murky that the diver can see no further than an arm's length; apart from air tanks, powerful torches are vital, as well as several knives (which may be needed to cut a way out of the embrace of a trawl net), fins and a wet or dry suit.

It can take a while to get established as a commercial diver, especially for those who do not have additional technical skills useful to employers. Pay is always by the day, with lowest rates for inland/offshore work and the highest earnings for those employed in the North Sea.

There are four basic training standards in the UK Diving Regulations for commercial divers: Parts I and II apply offshore, and Parts III and IV apply inland/inshore. Every year, commercial divers also have to pass a medical examination by an HSE-approved doctor. Training information, and a list of HSE-recognised courses, is available from IMCA. A Part I course costs around £5,000, inshore courses less.

The Royal Navy and the police carry out their own training programmes for their divers.

The highest earnings for professional sports diving instructors are in the warmer waters of Australia. In Thailand, earnings are equivalent to around £20,000, and can involve training local divers to work on oil rigs. Any country close to the equator, with year-round tourism, offers more work than seasonal areas, such as the Mediterranean. It helps to be able to speak one or more tourist languages: German or Japanese, for instance. Instructors may be employed full-time by a diving school, or work freelance using a school's facilities to teach, bringing in customers and taking half the profits.

Most sports diving instructors become qualified through one of the two major associations, both based in the USA but with schools worldwide. They are the professional Association of Diving Instructors (PADI), PO Box 25010, San Ana, California 92799–5010 (the largest) and the National Association of Underwater Instructors, PO Box 14650 Montclair, California 91763–1150. Dive schools that give PADI or NUI instruction are listed in the Yellow Pages, but there is a limited number of centres offering Diving Instructor courses, which may have to be taken abroad. Instructors normally take up diving as a hobby at first, through a sub-aqua club (addresses of clubs are available through the British Sub-Aqua Club, BSAC). The diving qualifications gained at BSAC amateur level can be converted to PADI Instructor III level.

In holiday resorts the diving instructor is highly respected ('they worship you' is how one instructor put it) – and the female instructors rarely have to carry their own air tanks.

Driving Instructor

CONTACT: Write for ADI Starter Pack, available from Driving Standards Agency, Stanley House, 56 Talbot Street, Nottingham NG1 5GU; price £2.50, includes application form

EARNINGS: From £250 to £350 per week

SKILLS: Full driving licence must have been held for four years; patience, tact, ability to inspire confidence and give clear instruction

With dual-control cars, some of the more hair-raising stories of being driven through walls and under lorries by petrified novice drivers have become legends of the past. But a driving instructor does need plenty of patience – even if it is all a sham and there is a monumental explosion of pent-up feeling back at home at the end of the day. Some instructors, on the other hand, become monosyllabic, to the fury of their spouses, because they have been talking for hours to their pupils.

Of course it is important to be a good driver, able to read the road ahead and anticipate events so that the pupil has several seconds for the instructions to sink in and be acted upon – before going through the red light. People who do not drive very well themselves would obviously find it very difficult to teach driving. It is also important to be able to instruct – there is no point in being the world's most expert driver if you cannot pass it on.

Pupils come in all shapes and ages, from the eager young seventeen-year-old lad who thinks he knows it all, to the middle-aged married matrons thrilled by the prospect of emancipation when they no longer have to ask anyone for a lift. Getting through the test is more a question of getting round safely with the prospect of improving skills later, so the demon driver has to be taught test-sense.

Whereas test examiners have to be stand-offish towards learners, instructors get involved with them, finding out what kind of people they are and the best way to teach them, whether they can be pushed hard, or whether to take things more slowly.

The number of lessons pupils need vary; an average is 40 to 50. A concerned and committed instructor is more likely to keep pupils than one who is not prepared to establish a rapport, and whose customers may drift off.

Most driving instructors work alone or through a driving school under a franchise scheme; recommendation is an important way of attracting new business. Rates for lessons are lower than those charged by the bigger schools that need to charge VAT.

The Department of Transport's qualification standards for driving instructors have risen, weeding out those who are not up to the mark, but the demand for expert tuition has also grown, so career prospects are good for those who do qualify.

The Department of Transport controls the examinations for registration as an Approved Driving Instructor, but does not offer any training courses. Fees are charged for each examination and for registration: Part I – written examination (£50), a single paper of 100 questions, with choice of three answers on each, on safety, driving techniques and driving tuition; Part II – practical test of driving ability (£55); Part III – practical test of instructional ability (£55); registration (£180) renewable every four years. There is a time limit of two calendar years to complete the training – if you fail to complete Part III within the time period you have to start all over again. A licence to give instruction (under instruction from an Approved Driving Instructor) during training costs £85 and is applied for after completing Parts I and II. The British School of Motoring offers a three- to six-month course for £1645 (1994), or £1995 including travel and accommodation. BSM driving instructors are self-employed, operating under a franchise agreement. There is a fixed franchise fee, but a car is provided. The average charge for a lesson is £14 and as you can work from 6.30 am to 7.30 pm seven days a week, earnings (minus car and/or franchise costs) can be high.

Embalmer

CONTACT: British Institute of Embalmers, Anubis House,
          21c Station Road, Knowle, Solihull, West Midlands
          B93 0HL; 01564 778991

SALARY: £15,000 to £16,000, or £15 to £50 per case

SKILLS: GCE O level/GCSE pass in English and Maths or
          nursing qualifications; age 17 or over

Not a lot of people know this, but most dead bodies are automatically embalmed – though it is not the kind of embalming practised by the ancient Egyptians. Modern embalming is a different process, used in the American Civil War and then taken up throughout America and Canada. So, like the 'funeral directors' who replaced the 'undertakers', it is a transatlantic import.

It is a necessary one though, and normally included as part of the funeral director's attendance services for the benefit of the employees as well as the relatives of the dead person. You very often have to wait for a week or more to be buried or cremated, especially if you choose to die on the wrong day of the week, for local authority staff do not work on Friday afternoons or at weekends. About 80 per cent of bodies are cremated now, so they have to be kept on the funeral director's premises until the local crematorium is ready to take them.

They may be kept in a fridge to stop deterioration, but are more likely to be embalmed, which is an inexpensive process and makes the bodies easier to handle and also better to look at if relatives or friends want to view them.

The aims of embalming are preservation, presentation and 'sanitisation'. Preservation was not so necessary in the days when bodies were buried only a day or two after death, before smells had time to develop, but with the longer waiting times nowadays, embalming or refrigeration has become essential, especially if the weather is hot (in hot countries without local authority staff bodies are disposed of quickly to avoid extra distress to relatives). Presentation is concerned with appearance, so that the dead person looks as normal as possible with natural colouring and as though asleep, in case relatives wish to view. If the person has been killed in an accident, or died after an operation, or undergone a post-mortem, wounds are stitched and signs of death removed as far as possible. Hair may be combed, and make-up applied – though this can cause problems if the final effect is nothing like the person in life. There is a special two-week 'restorative art' course held in Paris.

Sanitisation is really the *raison d'être* of modern embalming: to prepare a dead human body scientifically so that it will not become unsanitary or dangerous to the health of others before its final disposal. It is to protect the health of their staff against infection that undertakers normally carry it out routinely.

Modern embalmers simply withdraw some of the blood and fill the circulatory system with preservative chemicals (William and John Hunter, the great Scottish anatomists, had a part in developing the methods). The process, which also stops rigor mortis, takes about an hour, and is done in a special operating room.

Courses in embalming are held on a block or day-release basis by a number of schools and registered tutors and cost from around £250 for a part-time day release modular course (the usual way of learning) lasting 16 months to two years. A list of schools and tutors is available from the British Institute of Embalmers. Subjects covered include anatomy, physiology, pathology and bacteriology as well as embalming, with both theoretical and practical tuition. There are also correspondence courses. Embalming is often taken up by ex-nurses, and the work may take place on the funeral director's premises, or involve travelling around, occasionally overseas. Larger funeral directors employ embalmers on a full-time basis, but embalmers can also be self-employed, working for several companies.

Falconer

CONTACT: British Falconers Club, Home Farm, Hints,
Nr Tamworth, Staffordshire B78 3DW

SALARY: No fixed salaries

SKILLS: Understanding of wildlife; absolute patience when
dealing with animals; solitary disposition; acceptance of hunting as a leisure activity

Once there were falconers mewing up their birds at every great house in the country. Flying falcons are still an attraction at special events and tourist venues, where we like to be reminded of our medieval past. There are even centres dedicated to the conservation of birds of prey where free-flying displays are a daily feature. Now falconry in its true sense – as a hunting sport – is carried out mainly by amateurs with their own birds of prey. The quarry includes hares, rabbits, grey squirrels, game birds in season and other species not protected by the Wildlife and Countryside Act 1981.

Some of these amateurs who have a collection can get their birds to work for their living protecting military airbases and civilian airfields against bird strike (flocks of birds that cause an aircraft to crash if they get sucked into the jet engines). They scare off the plovers and other birds that like to feed on the grass next to the runways. They are sub-contracted to do the same kind of job on rubbish tips, too, scaring off gulls, and occasionally scaring pigeons around high-rise buildings. It is not very regular, but you'd be paid £50 per session (from two hours to a day).

There are very few professional falconers in the country, employed by people who own birds of prey to train the birds to hunt or taking groups out hunting. There are several falconry schools who employ experienced falconers to train owners to hunt their birds or provide holidays. Owners come from all over the world, from places as far apart as America and Zimbabwe (where falconry is controlled by apprenticeship and licensing regulations), Australia and Mexico.

Public displays are currently being given by a limited number of skilled professionals and amateurs; so there could be openings for skilled falconers with their own birds in the leisure industry. (We are not talking about the inexpert 'owl on a piece of string' flying display or birds exhibited in cages.)

The initial outlay for buying a government-registered bird (birds of prey are strictly controlled by legislation), plus accommodation and equipment, including not only the glove for the owner and hood and jesses for the bird, but also a deep freeze for the day-old male chicks from the hatcheries used as food, is around £1000. Birds (which are captive-bred) are cheaper at the end of the season, which begins in the early autumn after moulting and lasts through the winter, then starts again with a spring season. The birds hunt grouse, pheasant and partridge in autumn; rabbits and rooks in winter.

As you gain more experience you would progress to working with other species of birds of prey – from kestrel to buzzard, working with owls, peregrine, goshawk, sparrow-hawk and finally golden eagle.

Joining a club like the British Falconers Club is a good start, as it can recommend courses and give advice on buying, and on legislation.

Firefighter

CONTACT: The County Fire Headquarters

SALARY: From £12,897

SKILLS: Aged between 18 and 30; height, between 5ft 6in
            (1.68m) and 6ft 4in (1.93m); high level of physical
            fitness; good eyesight without contact lenses or
            glasses; no gastric or rheumatic complaints, skin
            diseases, claustrophobia, vertigo; good hearing; abil-
            ity to work in a team

Question: Why would a fire engine be driving at speed away from a fire? *Answer:* Because the crew has gone to look for a source of water. If the fire is in a hay-filled barn in the middle of a field, the supply of water can run out quickly, and the nearest lake, pond or stream will suddenly become vitally important.

A firefighter's first barn fire may be spectacular, and end in nothing but a few charred posts in the ground – and a large bill for the insurance company. But the crews attending fire engines are much more pleased if they can bring the situation under control and keep the structure of the building safe with their water jets, even if the bales stacked inside smoulder away to nothing. It can be a long job, too, keeping an eye on the barn contents, looking for the sudden flickers of flame as an apparently dead fire springs back into life.

In the countryside, the crew manning the fire appliances are likely to be fully trained retained part-timers, ever ready to down tools and get themselves to the fire station in Linford Christie time as soon as their bleeper sounds.

In towns the fire crew is permanent, with long periods of waiting for an emergency, and sudden spurts of action when they are called to a 'shout', which could be anything from a road traffic accident (RTA) – or a cow in a ditch (the lifting equipment has many uses) – to a major blaze in a paper store. During times of 'inactivity' there is plenty to do – maintaining the equipment, escorting groups of visitors round and teaching them about fire safety, advising local businesses about fire hazards and, above all, training. There are regular training sessions for both part-time and permanent crews, to ensure that responses are automatic, to keep everyone fit, and to keep up to date with new techniques.

There's new technology to help: thermal imaging cameras to help find fire victims in thick smoke, protective suits for when there are chemical spills, computers that hold the latest information about those chemicals, their effects and how to deal with them, and street plans and details of high-risk buildings. Work goes on all the time on improving the technology: most of the larger brigades have research and development departments that both test existing equipment and work on designing new equipment and clothing.

Each county's fire service carries out its own training programme, normally of 12 weeks at a training school, followed by a two-week breathing apparatus course. This is when men who like beards or bushy sideburns discover why they are not allowed. You also need to learn how to drive the powerful fire engines (or, correctly, appliances).

Entrants may be graduates or non-graduates, but all must have the initial training, which is followed by on-the-job training and the continuous in-service training. There are good opportunities for promotion. A firefighter can rise to Leading Firefighter and then Station Officer (earning up to £22,000) within five years, after passing the necessary Fire Service examinations.

Those promoted to officer level take a course at the national Fire Service College in Gloucestershire, which covers management skills as well as firefighting. There are also courses in fire safety, road traffic procedures and breathing apparatus instruction. Senior officers in management posts are given management and command training courses.

Fire officers can also gain professional qualifications in Fire Engineering and study for membership of the Institution of Fire Engineers, which is open to both full-time and part-time firefighters.

Guide Dog Trainer

CONTACT: Guide Dogs for the Blind Association,
Hillfields, Burghfield, Reading, Berkshire RG7 3YG;
01734 835555

SALARY: From £7780 per annum

SKILLS: Experience with animals, as well as work/social
experience with adults of various backgrounds.
Robust physique; good health record; articulate and
confident in dealing with groups of people (as well
as dogs). Full UK driving licence. Educated to GCSE
standard (or equivalent) including English, maths
and a science subject

How does an over-enthusiastic, embarrassingly friendly, bounding Labrador, normally attached to an anxiously apologising owner, become such a paragon of virtue as a guide dog?

The answer lies with the puppy walkers and guide dog trainers who teach good manners early and choose the dogs whose characters will suit their work. A dog – not always a Labrador; other breeds are used as well – stays with its Puppy Walker until it is nine months to a year old and is then handed over to the Guide Dog Trainer.

The first task of the trainer is to get to know the dog, taking it for walks and giving it obedience training. During this time the dog is assessed for suitability as a guide dog; special considerations have to be taken into account, such as 'body sensitivity'. Dogs whose body sensitivity is high have to be rejected because they are the type who go too far out of their way to avoid obstacles in their path – not very convenient for a blind or visually impaired owner in a hurry.

Once the trainer has decided the dog is suitable, more serious training is given in walking at a steady speed, responding to voice commands and getting used to the harness the dog will eventually wear as it guides its owner.

The dog normally stays with its trainer for seven to nine months and there the responsibility ends, for the more advanced training is undertaken by a Mobility Instructor. It is at this stage that the dog learns about judging height, width and safety situations as they are related to their owners holding the harness, and the Mobility Instructor also helps the new owners to get used to handling their dogs.

Some Guide Dog Trainers are recruited from the Association's kennel staff, who normally live in at one of the Association's seven centres. They care for the dogs, being responsible for feeding and exercising, and also meet and help their blind owners when they are taking over their dogs. Applicants (and there are many) should be at least 18 with good personality and liking for people – as well as for the four-footed friends.

To qualify as a Mobility Instructor you need to undertake a three-year apprenticeship (age limit is 18 or above); the salary for a qualified Mobility Instructor is comparable with teachers' salaries.

Herbalist

CONTACT: National Institute of Medical Herbalists, 9 Palace Gate, Exeter, Devon EX1 1JA (please send sae); 01392 426022

EARNINGS: About £10 to £15 per half-hour consultation

SKILLS: Sense of vocation and genuine interest in helping to relieve suffering; for training, GCE O-level/GCSE passes including Chemistry and Biology (A-level passes preferred)

Herbal medicine has been around for centuries, perhaps even longer than acupuncture. The first herbal guides were written in Assyria and China and the art was practised in India, Egypt, Greece and Rome. Though the theories of physicians such as Hippocrates and Galen seem wide of the mark today, for they believed that the herbs should be used to balance four 'elements' in the body, skills in herbal remedies spread throughout the civilised world, mingling with the ancient knowledge handed down in communities and families.

In England, in the seventeenth century, Nicholas Culpeper published his famous Herbal, and it is still consulted now. He intended the book to be used to help in treating poor people effectively and cheaply, with herbs growing in the wild. Meanwhile the physicians and druggists were prescribing more expensive mineral purges and bleeding to treat illness – often on the 'kill or cure' principle. And the old-style herbalists were slowly overtaken by the popularity of new synthetic drugs developed as early as the 1850s.

In recent years, of course, the dangers of synthetic drugs have been realised and there is a new surge of interest in herbal medicine, which emphasises that a part of the whole plant (such as leaves, berries or root) should be used in treating illness, to prevent the side-effects that can result when the active ingredient is isolated.

Like other practitioners of alternative medicines, herbalists spend time on their consultations, finding the underlying cause of the problem, giving advice on diet and making up prescriptions for tablets, liquids or lotions that may include several herbs. Conditions treated include asthma, hay fever, arthritis, rheumatism, heart conditions and tension.

There is a new three- to four-year full-time (or up to six years part-time) course for a BSc/BSc Honours in Herbal Medicine at Middlesex University (Enfield Campus) with Licentiate Membership of the National Institute of Medical Herbalists. A four-year full-time course, and four-year tutorial course are offered by the School of Phytotherapy (Herbal Medicine), Bucksteep Manor, Bodle Street Green, Hailsham BN27 4RJ. Entry requirements are good GCSE/O-level passes including English and two A-level passes, one of which should be science based. Fees for the full-time course are around £3600 per year; the courses lead to membership of the National Institute of Medical Herbalists.

A two-year London-based postgraduate diploma course in Chinese Herbal Medicine is offered by the School of Chinese Herbal Medicine (Midsummer Cottage Clinic, Nether Westcote, Kingham, Oxfordshire OX7 6SD; 01993 830419). The course is for second- and third-year students and graduates of acupuncture and herbal medicine colleges, acupuncturists, practising herbalists and doctors. Fees are £1150 per year.

Jeweller

CONTACT: British Jewellers' Association, 10 Vyse Street, Birmingham B18 6LT; 0121 236 2657

SALARY: From around £180 to £300 a week

SKILLS: Manual dexterity; artistic ability

As a jeweller you may not become as famous as Fabergé or Lalique, but you would be working with the same precious metals of gold, platinum and silver, and beautiful gemstones. The finished article may be a simple wedding ring, pair of cufflinks or earrings or a diamond and sapphire brooch or necklace for a customer with thousands of pounds (or dollars, or yen) to spend.

The large jewellery companies, with shops all over the country, employ craftsmen to make up the pieces in their own factories. There are also manufacturers who sell jewellery to the retailers, without having any shops of their own. The design of factory-made jewellery is mainly traditional, or copies of successful work by other jewellers. Some of the larger shops have their own designers, who make up special commissions for customers. This gives them the chance to play around with some fabulously valuable stones.

The designer working for a retailer has to tailor the look of the jewellery to the shop's own style; the artist–craftsman working for himself or herself has far more freedom to create pieces of jewellery that are individual and unique.

Making jewellery needs a steady hand and the patience of a perfectionist. The craftsman sits at a work bench with a skin hanging underneath the work to catch the precious metal filings (all sent back to the bullion dealers) and a gas flame within reach to heat the metal so that it can be bent into shape. In a factory the work may consist of making the setting or mounting the stones, rather than making the whole piece of jewellery from start to finish. Gold wire, shanks for rings, ear clips and screws, pins for brooches and even stone settings may be bought in from a supplier. Castings are made of complete settings, so that replicas can be set with different stones, or of separate details, such as bracelet segments or patterned shapes to be combined into a finished piece.

A designer–craftsman, working alone or with a craftsman making up the designs in his or her workshop, is rather like a couturier in the fashion business, producing individual work commissioned by customers or for sale. The work may include not only jewellery but also chains of office or silver pieces such as goblets or cigarette boxes, ash-trays and presentation trophies. Silversmithing can be combined with exciting special effects using enamelling, as seen in the work of Fabergé.

Craftsmen who do mass-produced work for manufacturers can take a one-year pre-entry course at a college, followed by a four-year apprenticeship; no special qualifications are necessary. The three major schools of jewellery are the Birmingham School of Jewellery, Branston Street, Birmingham; London Guildhall University, Central House, 59 Whitechapel High Street, London E1 7PS; Kent Institute of Art and Design, Rochester, Kent.

Designer craftsmen take a three- or four-year full-time degree course, with work experience in the jewellery industry included as part of a sandwich course; entry to college follows a one-year foundation course at art school, with minimum A-level entry requirements. Courses in design combined with jewellery and silversmithing are held at a number of colleges and universities, and can include business studies – useful for those intending to 'go it alone'. Graduates may also run workshops for large companies, work as studio managers or go into public relations work, retailing or gallery work. After a few quiet years, the jewellery industry is now in a healthy state with salaries of £30,000 a possibility.

Jockey

CONTACT: Recruiting Offiicer, Racing and Thoroughbred
            Breeding Training Board (RTBTB), PO Box 21,
            Newmarket, Suffolk CB8 9BL; 01638 560743
            The British Racing School, Snailwell Road,
            Newmarket, Suffolk CB8 7NU
            The Northern Racing School, Rossington Hall,
            Great North Road, Doncaster DN11 0HN

EARNINGS: *Riding fee* Flat racing: £58. National Hunt: £80
            (1994/95 rates). Plus a percentage of the prize
            money

SKILLS: Age 16 to 18; under 9 to 9½ stone; physical strength;
            riding skills an advantage

There can't be many thrills that equal the experience of being the jockey who wins one of the great races, such as the Grand National. The face of the successful jockey, interviewed on television immediately afterwards and often struggling to hold back tears of emotion, shows that.

Throughout the year there are hundreds of other races taking place at racecourses all over the country that don't make it to the television screen and where winning is what the jockey's job is all about, rather than being a celebrity. Jockeys can ride in either flat races or National Hunt races (over fences, in steeplechases like the Grand National or in hurdle races). The obstacles in National Hunt racing make it more exciting for the spectator but more hazardous for horse and jockey. Racing 'over the sticks' goes on during the winter, lasting from August to June. Flat racing has a shorter season, from late March to the beginning of November.

Most jockeys ride in either flat or National Hunt races only, although some do both; and the same applies to the stables who train the horses. Some train steeplechasers, hurdlers, and horses for the flat, but most specialise. There are many more National Hunt jockeys than flat-race riders, but the

National Hunt jockeys come into it from various routes – perhaps from flat racing, or as amateur riders who have had experience in riding in the point-to-point races organised by local hunts. National Hunt jockeys can be heavier than the rules regarding weights carried in flat racing allow, so many trainees who have become too heavy for flat racing switch over to National Hunt.

Training is by apprenticeship: up to age 24 for a flat-race jockey or 25 for a 'jump' jockey, or earlier if he or she has ridden 75 winners. The British Racing School at Newmarket and Northern Racing School at Doncaster run free ten-week courses for 16- to 18-year olds during which they learn how to handle thoroughbred race horses and the techniques of racing. The 9-stone weight limit may be raised to 9½ stone when there is a shortage of applicants of the right weight (people are getting heavier). Good, keen riders may also be accepted over the weight limit.

School leavers are advised to apply to a training stables first for at least three weeks' work experience before applying to the school for an interview, though if necessary they can be placed by the School. Often the stables will agree to take them back after the course on an apprenticeship. Names of trainers are to be found in *Horses in Training* or the *Directory of the Turf* (which includes studs and trainers in Ireland and France), available through libraries or bookshops. You can also try Yellow Pages for the main racing centres like Newmarket or Lambourn.

Trainee jockeys start with hard work in the stables, where they work with the stable-lads caring for the horses, mucking out, grooming, feeding, providing fresh water and keeping the yard clean. They take on responsibility for two or three horses and exercise them on the gallops. When the horses are entered for races, there is the chance to go to the racecourse with them and lead them around the parade ring.

Trainee jockeys often live in at the stables, usually in a hostel, working a long day, with afternoons free and about one day off every two weeks. For those who make it as professional jockeys the work load is heavy too, with a great deal of travelling, both within the UK and to races abroad. Those who are not successful enough with winners may continue to work for the race-horse trainers as stable-lads.

Kissogram Girl/Man

CONTACT: Local agency, through Yellow Pages

EARNINGS: Around £23 to £30 (topless) for an appearance

SKILLS: Good looks; age up to late 20s; acting skills, usually some acting experience; extrovert

Kissograms are all about the infliction of excruciating embarrassment on the hapless victim, to the merry laughter of so-called friends and family. That is why one of the most popular is the policewoman, allegedly sometimes perpetrated in the local nick where the real coppers obligingly give the conspirators proper police badges to use in their foul deed. The police lady makes her arrest, makes an accusation of some crime such as an out-of-date road tax disc, gets her subject thoroughly wound up – and then proceeds to take off her uniform down to the sexy frilly undies ... No wonder the act goes down well in the cop shop! Then, following the normal kissogram routine, she sits on the subject's knee, gives him lots of kisses, sings 'Happy Birthday' or some other appropriate ditty and reads out her telegram message.

Other characters include the schoolgirl, French maid, nurse, belly-dancer and big, fat rolypoly lady (plump, young and good-looking). The male roles are Tarzan, gorilla, policeman, doctor, Superman and the drunk (imagine the embarrassment!).

You need to be outgoing to be able to rustle up a party spirit in the crowd and get everyone involved when the atmosphere may be flagging, perhaps getting all the family together for a snapshot; you may have to do the act in front of a large audience or just two people.

The whole performance takes about 15 minutes, so kissogrammers may be able to fit in more than one in an evening – though the girls avoid stag nights after 10 pm, when the participants are likely to be dancing on the tables themselves.

Most engagements are for birthdays and anniversaries, as well as office leaving and retirement parties, Round Table social evenings or product promotions, and they take place, except for office parties, on Saturdays and during the evenings.

Costumes and cars for transport are normally supplied, and perhaps a gift to mollify the kissogrammee; maybe the garter from the lady's leg. Sometimes, though, petrol costs have to come out of the fee, which may be around £10 more for a non-local engagement. The agencies sometimes recruit through press advertisements and their staff are mostly part time, though there may be some working full time, and are likely to be mainly 'up-and-coming' actors and actresses. In London, agencies may expect a full strip, and a certain amount of sordidness has crept into the business, but elsewhere the emphasis is on fun, and an act that wouldn't frighten the horses – or children.

Long Haul Lorry Driver

CONTACT: Road Transport Industry Training Board,
            (RTITB) Services Ltd, York House, Empire Way,
            Wembley, Middlesex HA9 0RT; 0181 902 8880

SALARY: From around £8,000 to over £30,000 per annum
            plus subsistence allowance (up to £25 per night)

SKILLS: Physical fitness; proficient driver, engineer and
            navigator; able to take responsibility for valuable
            cargoes; Class C and E HGV licence

The Gulf States in the Middle East, even (rarely) Pakistan, are among the stops at the end of the long-distance roads. From worrying about traffic jams at Dover, there's the problem instead of camels wandering across the road at night in the desert. And in between there are the autobahns of Germany, the poverty of some of the East European countries, where your food may be stolen and the petrol queues may be four days long, and the excitement of Istanbul and the friendliness of the people of Turkey. There are border posts, where your smattering of German, Turkish and Arabic comes in handy, and where belongings are unceremoniously searched, or dogs used to sniff out forbidden whisky or drugs.

Meeting other drivers from Sweden, Norway, Austria, Bulgaria, Poland – from all points of the compass – gives a chance of comradeship with other nationalities that the tourist never experiences. Wives can accompany drivers, but not to Saudi Arabia, and there can be the chance of a couple of days off for sightseeing once the load is delivered.

Trips take around three weeks to the Middle East, or more if an engine gives trouble, interspersed with ten to 14 days at home. It is a situation that can put a strain on marriages.

During that three weeks the truck is the driver's home, with air conditioning in summer time and night heaters for the winter, and the World Service on short-wave radio for companionship. It is up to the driver to cope with border problems or engine blowouts, and to carry the responsibility for the safety of his load. There is a lot of mileage involved, and the satisfaction is in getting to the destination and delivering the load. Then it's back through countries such as Yugoslavia, picking up another load, maybe of furniture, on the way.

The European routes, which include Russia and Greece, are more competitive in terms of deadlines – even the excuse of a breakdown may not save the firm from losing a contract through late delivery. Salaries vary widely and can depend on whether you are hauling a hazardous or temperature-controlled load, bulk tank freight or small parcels.

To drive an artic (articulated lorry) you need a Class C (rigid vehicle) plus E (trailer) HGV licence; you cannot drive any heavy goods vehicle until you are aged 21. A young HGV Driver's Scheme for young people between the ages of 16 and 20 who are already employed by a company is currently on hold but may become operational when the economy improves. Training at one of the special schools to gain an HGV licence can be expensive, depending on how much training is needed – normally ten days at around £1100. RTITB Services Ltd has a list of approved schools. Training schools are also listed in the Yellow Pages. Many companies will not employ drivers until they are over 25, for insurance reasons. Some drivers own their 'rig' (around £70,000 to £80,000 to buy). They are an independent breed.

Loss Adjuster

CONTACT: Chartered Institute of Loss Adjusters, Manfield
House, 376 Strand, London WC2R 0LR;
0171 240 1496

SALARY: Around £10,000 per annum at start of training with
degree or other qualifications

SKILLS: Integrity; good powers of observation; social skills

It has to be admitted that loss adjusting is sailing pretty close
to the wind for those who jib at accountancy. The Association's final exams have a nasty section concerned with
double-entry bookkeeping, trial balances, profit and loss
accounts, costing systems, bankruptcy and that kind of thing.
However, examinees are also expected to know about more
diverse subjects, such as burglary, theft, Guatemala Protocol
1971, goods in transit by road, rail or air, the cultivation and
harvesting of crops, modern stock farming and spontaneous
combustion.

Such a range of interests and possible attendant disasters
can only be found in the insurance business. A loss adjuster is
a claims specialist, working independently of the insurance
companies who have their own claims staff, but who call on
the services of loss adjusters to settle contentious or complex
claims. Sometimes it may mean providing objective arbitra-
tion on claims, or sorting out intricate claims in which several
insurance underwriters are sharing a risk.

Loss adjusting firms tend to specialise, so that they have an
in-depth knowledge of one particular subject. Their responsibility is to ascertain the proper liability of an insurer for a loss.
They must investigate the cause of a loss, confirm that the
conditions set out in the insurance policy have been properly
observed and find out what kind of claim the policyholder will
be making. It can mean investigating what caused a loss –
which might be a collapsed building, a chemical explosion or
a company's loss of profits – and getting statements or

physical evidence to use later in negotiations on behalf of the claimant's insurers. So the loss adjuster acts rather like a private detective, sleuthing around picking up clues after, perhaps, a warehouse fire in the middle of winter. Disasters such as serious floods can lead to sudden rushes of work, and at all times the loss adjuster needs not only knowledge and training, but also a good relationship with the many people from different backgrounds encountered during enquiries into losses. Definitely not a boring job.

Originally, loss adjusters were used by the insurance companies, mainly to handle claims for fire and explosion. Over the 200 years they have been in existence their interests have widened to include flood and storm damage, theft, transit losses, failures on constructional contract sites (so an understanding of building methods is needed), factory failures, loss of profits, public liability, products liability, employers' liability, fidelity guarantees and personal accident claims. There are plenty of opportunities to work overseas on either a temporary or permanent basis with firms that have international organisations.

Entry into the profession may be at trainee level, with private study towards passing the Institute's exams. Applications can be made to individual firms by A-level school leavers or graduates. Qualified surveyors, engineers, accountants, solicitors and officials from the claims department of insurance companies all have skills that are particularly relevant to loss adjusting.

There are also people in the trade who are average adjusters, with their own association. Their name does not imply that they are neither brilliantly clever nor stupendously useless – simply that they deal only in marine loss.

Mail Courier

CONTACT: Local courier companies (Yellow Pages) or international companies, such as DHL and TNT Skypak

EARNINGS: Around £12,000 per annum for a van driver

SKILLS: Driving licence; common sense; integrity

Helmeted and leathered, or lycra-ed, the couriers in London weave through the traffic on their bikes with impressive urgency. They operate between offices, carrying documents of all kinds, plus photographs, tapes, transparencies and copy for magazines and newspapers, film, samples, floppy disks, advertising material – anything that needs to be urgently 'biked' from one part of town to another.

It's an advantage to have a knowledge of the roads and geography of the area, but otherwise no special qualifications are needed, except a driving licence and commonsense – more useful here than A levels and degrees. Many couriers are self-employed, using their own motorbikes, vans, or high-speed pushbikes with colourful high-speed Lycra gear to match. A self-employed inner-city pushbiker can earn £300 to £400 per week; a motorbiker, who may have to go from London to Leicester and back, up to £600.

They report to the courier office in the morning, and then, checking back to base with their mobile phones and radios, are kept busy all day.

The motorbikes supplied by the courier companies to their staff are sensible, economical standard models – nothing too powerful or expensive.

Companies range from small local courier services, to large international organisations, with offices not only throughout the UK, but around the world as well. Those working for the large companies use the company's vans, instead of their own. Couriers who take packages from one town to another deliver them to the local representatives, who then take over delivery to the recipient. The same usually applies to destinations overseas.

Couriers who fly regularly to Europe take the packages through the airport to the local courier representatives. They work on a rota system, flying one week to Dublin, for instance, and the next week to Madrid.

Most material sent by air express is unaccompanied, but sometimes documents are of such a nature that they must have a personal escort; the courier can speed up the process of getting them through customs and other checks and into the local courier office, which takes over the responsibility of getting them to their destination. The courier normally flies straight back on the next available flight, which is no problem at the major airports. In some of the more far-flung countries, though, the next available connecting flight could be a week away, leaving the courier temporarily stranded.

Documents going overseas could include tenders for important work contracts, legal and business materials, oil-related companies sending the results of their research and other important documents. Couriers are checked for their security and integrity by the courier companies, and are normally recruited on recommendation.

Although fax machines could affect courier services, since they can transmit even hand-written or drawn material along the telephone lines, there has been only a small drop in demand for this reason. The boom time was in the 1980s, when couriers might have earned up to £800 per week – and now they are hoping to get back on the fast track again.

Market Trader

CONTACT: Local markets; Association of Private Market
            Operators, 4 Worrygoose Lane, Rotherham,
            South Yorkshire S60 4AD; 01709 700072

SALARY: From £10,000 to £25,000

SKILLS: Affable – good with customers, even difficult ones;
            able to put up with bad weather conditions, and get
            up early

If the climate really is hotting up (or cooling down) the people who will be most aware of it are market traders, who set up their stalls come wind, snow, rain or heat wave. When you can't afford to lose a day's business, only a hurricane will keep you at home. And you'd expect to start out before the first radio weather forecasts: a flash (stall display) needs to be set up by 9 am. This means being in the market to start unloading the goods by 7 to 7.30 am, after a journey of perhaps two hours, depending on how far away from home the market is.

Traders selling fresh meat, fruit and vegetables will first have visited the wholesalers to buy the produce; an even earlier start!

Most casuals, as newcomers are known, would not expect to begin with a fresh produce stall – these are popular lines, and markets would have enough regular stalls selling fresh goods. (Casuals also need an extra early morning start, to be first in the queue for a vacant stall.) Beginners are best with lines such as clothing (from manufacturers who've produced more than they need), greetings cards, branded snack packets, sweets, canned drinks; or unusual lines that will not be competing with other stalls, to increase the chance of getting on to a market.

Markets are operated by local authorities or private operators, or are to be found at shows, fairs and special events; it's worth doing research on those within tolerable travelling distance. Rents are from £1.80 per day in a council-run market (difficult to get on to) and around £8 to £10 per day during the week; £15 to £20 at weekends in private markets. Never pay rent on a stall in advance.

Apart from goods, bought from wholesalers, manufacturers, cash-and-carry stores or auctions, the market trader needs a vehicle, probably a secondhand van (cost around £6000) unless the goods will fit into the boot of a car. To avoid a wasted day's trading, which may never be made up, the vehicle must be reliable.

Goods of decent quality at competitive prices, a pleasant attitude to customers (give a refund, rather than have a slanging match), and a regular stall, help to build up steady sales. The stall (usually provided by the market) must look attractive but needs plenty of cover against rain and wind, which can ruin stock.

For those who don't want to work on an outdoor stall, there are indoor markets where you may eventually be allotted a pitch, or take over the tenancy of a stall (around £10,000; best handled by a solicitor).

Pricing needs to be carefully assessed: profits have to take into account vehicle running costs, stationery, rents, insurance, income tax and (especially if the goods are high-cost items) VAT.

Two magazines with useful info and sources of goods are *Marketeer and Discount Trader* (free at markets) and *Market Trader*, from newsagents. Details of consumer rights are given in *Market Trader Annual*. There's information for beginners in *The Guide to Market Trading* by David Glasby, £1.50 from Media Magazines, Northampton, and *Running Your Own Market Stall* by Dave J Hardwick (Kogan Page).

Market traders, like high street retailers, have to compete with out-of-town shopping centres but they are popular with customers who enjoy their chattiness in contrast with the impersonal atmosphere in most supermarkets. The best season is October to Christmas.

Massage Therapist

CONTACT: British Association of Beauty Therapy and Cosmetology Ltd, Parabola House, Parabola Road, Cheltenham, Gloucestershire GL50 3AH; 01242 570284

SALARY: £25 to £30 per hour's session; £20 per hour (London rates)

SKILLS: Physical strength and stamina; interest in helping people

Those who have never seen a massage therapist in action at a health farm or sauna will probably remember countless scenes from films or television soap operas where beautiful women exchange gossip or over-plump gentlemen make business deals lying on a hard board, draped in a towel as their flesh is kneaded by the impassive masseur or masseuse.

Massage has become a popular part of the health and beauty routine, used to tone up muscles and joints, and help in overcoming aches and pains. It is not a new idea; the massage slave is often a feature of those early Roman epic films, too. Like so many natural health notions, it originated in China.

A massage therapist needs to have an understanding of anatomy and physiology, and of how the muscles work, and to develop a sensitive touch when carrying out the routine. Training in massage also includes electrical treatments to stimulate muscles, known as faradism, electrical gyratory massage, vacuum suction, infra-red radiant heat, ultra-violet lamp and 'galvanic' stimulation. Exercises, to tone up and slim down clients, are also included.

The clients who are treated by a massage therapist may be seeking relaxation or a better shape, or treatment after some kind of sporting injury. Massage is part of the all-round training of a beauty therapist, who will do facial as well as body massage.

Massage therapists work in beauty salons, slimming clubs, health farms, local authority-run sports centres, public swimming pools and saunas and in private practice massage therapy clinics.

There are now NVQ/SVQs in massage therapy, taken with core units that apply to all beauty therapy, which can be taken up to Level 3; units at this level include aromatherapy massage.

The Confederation of International Beauty Therapy and Cosmetology (CIBTAC) includes an examination for a Body Therapist Diploma as part of its beauty course syllabus; the 300-hour Body Therapist Diploma course includes body massage, figure analysis, exercises, electrical treatments, heat treatments and other subjects including business organisation.

A body massage and physical culture course gives basic training in body massage, figure care and development, fitness and general well-being and is designed for massage therapists who will be working in saunas, health clubs and Turkish baths. A health and beauty therapy course is designed for people who intend to work in health and beauty clubs, saunas and slimming salons, giving training in non-remedial massage. A Swedish massage course concentrates on remedial massage therapy, for those who want to work in sports clubs, health farms or in private practice.

The courses combine practical and theoretical training.

Fees for training depend on the centre providing the programme, and on how long it takes. Grants are not normally available, but CIBTAC suggests contacting your local education authority.

Model Maker

CONTACT: Colleges (as given below) or local model-making
            firms (in Yellow Pages)

SALARY: £300 to £350 per week, average

SKILLS: Imagination, though not artistic creativity; manual
            dexterity

If no one had made a model of the proposed National Gallery extension, the 'carbuncle' remark might never have been made, because it is not until a design is translated into three-dimensional form that people can get a good impression of how the finished result will look. The next National Gallery plan was much admired; the model on display showed just how the new building would fit in with its neighbours in Trafalgar Square.

It is not only the designs of architects that come alive to the layman in model form; the research and development departments of manufacturers making all kinds of items use models of their proposed new products to help their board of directors to decide whether to go ahead with the idea. The mock-up may not be to scale, or given anything more than a coat of grey paint, but being able to handle a rough prototype is more helpful than looking at a technical drawing.

Models can be used in marketing promotions, for wind-tunnel testing, and to illustrate civil engineering projects, such as bridges and motorway features, as well as office or domestic building plans.

While model making of this kind looks to the future, other models reflect the past: scale models of ships, cars, railway engines, aircraft, old houses. Museums, such as the National Maritime Museum, use model makers to make their displays, and here there is the chance for a little artistic creativity, in the construction of seascapes and other settings. Skills of the same kind are used in topographical models, such as the terrain and runways that seem to present hazards to the novice in a tank or flight simulator.

In a different field altogether are the special effects models used in films, including television advertisements (for which a freelance can earn £200 to £400 per day). Here the model maker's work might follow the designer far into the future in a sci-fi film, or be burned to the ground or blown to pieces in a dramatic piece of action that will look real on the screen – but at far less hazard and expense.

Model making has become a very diverse subject, from exact small-scale reproductions, to oil platform mock-ups, local authority projects and eye-catching displays – perhaps for a giant toadstool or a chef advertising a restaurant, designed to lure the public.

Although wood is used as the main material for model making during training, students also learn to work with plastics, metal and glass.

There are a number of model-making firms, and departments attached to large companies, such as civil engineers, and local authorities, as well as freelance model makers. The only firm offering apprenticeships (to 16- to 20-year-olds) is Thorp Modelmakers Ltd, 98 Gray's Inn Road, London WC1X 8AW. Apprentices start at around £100 per week. There are degree and HND courses at a number of colleges: Kent Institute of Art and Design, Rochester upon Medway College, Fort Pitt, Rochester, Kent; Design Studies Division, University of Hertfordshire, St Albans School of Art and Design, Hatfield Road, St Albans, Herts AL1 3RS; Bournemouth and Poole College of Art and Design, Wallisdown, Poole, Dorset BH12 5HH; Department of Fine Craftsmanship and Design, Rycote Wood College, Priest End, Thame, Oxfordshire OX9 2AF. BTEC courses are also offered at Barking College, Romford, Essex; Coventry Technical College, Butts, Coventry CV1 3GD and South Devon College, Newton Road, Torquay TQ2 5BY. Further details of college courses from Art and Design Admissions Registry (ADAR), Penn House, 9 Broad Street, Hereford HR4 9AP and BTEC, Central House, Upper Woburn Place, London WC1H 0HH.

Model making can lead to creating animations for television, where you could be responsible for writing stories, creating characters, filming and editing your own independently produced series; and to film work, with the Roger Rabbit and Aladdin type of cartoon animations.

Mushroom Farmer

CONTACT: Mushroom Growers Association, 2 St Pauls Street,
             Stamford, Lincolnshire PE9 2BE; 01780 66888

EARNINGS: Around £12,000–£15,000 per annum, self-employed

SKILLS: Physical fitness and good health; ability to work long
             hours, every day of the year; attention to detail

Mushrooms are shy about poking their little white heads above the ground unless the temperature is a steady 64 to 65°F (18°C). So there's a nice warm shed for the mushroom farmer to go to in winter; a cool one in summer.

The start-up costs of making your own compost are high, because the Environmental Protection Act 1990 means the operation must be entirely enclosed, using specialised machinery. So although it is more expensive, most farmers buy their compost ready sterilised from a supplier. They may also buy it ready-spawned. The cost of 6 tons of spawned compost, supplied in polythene-covered blocks, is around £525.

Those who make their own use straw, chicken litter or horse manure, and gypsum mixed together and damped down to produce a build-up of sterilising heat. The heap is then pasteurised in trays to kill off competing organisms, though not the micro-organisms needed by the mushrooms. After cooling, the compost is put in cases, covered with a layer of chalk and peat and spawned before being put in trays. Three weeks later the mushrooms appear and are cropped for three weeks, and then the compost is discarded, the shed is cleared and sterilised and the whole process starts again.

Meanwhile there are other sheds at different stages, with one coming 'on line' with more mushrooms ready to be picked. Mushroom farming is a seven days a week, 365 days a year commitment, so good planning is necessary for holidays. Unfortunately, basic costs have risen in recent years, while retail prices have remained the same in the face of competition from imports from the Dutch, Belgians, French and the Irish. The result has been some bankruptcies. Very small farmers can get a better price by delivering their own produce to local shops, selling to them at less than a wholesaler would charge, but at more than they would get from a wholesaler.

You don't have to live in the country to be a mushroom farmer; factory or industrial premises would be suitable and could have the advantage of more local retail outlets – but beware of disease and competing fungus potential. What is necessary are concrete floors, insulated sheds with temperature and humidity controls and racks. An alternative to sheds is woven polythene fitted on to hoops, with fibreglass insulation. Heating is needed in winter, and air conditioning to cool the air during hot weather. Mushrooms must have humid conditions for growing, so there is extra maintenance as damp is not kind to building materials. Five sheds, worked in rotation and producing about half a ton of mushrooms per week, is suitable for a mushroom farmer working alone. The biggest farms may have an area of one million square feet, but most of the 300 or so growers in this country are small; one acre of land is more than enough for a single person. The Ministry of Agriculture's advisory service, ADAS, will give help to beginners (at a cost).

Anyone starting in the business must first make sure that it is possible to sell the produce locally. In some areas the growers may cooperate in supplying the market, so it is worth doing some research before starting up in a particular area.

Disease can be a problem, but not a serious one if sheds are kept meticulously sterile. With millions of mushroom spores drifting about, there can be a health problem for the farmer who develops a sensitivity to them. Otherwise, mushroom farming is a fine, cosy indoor farming life.

Nature Reserve Warden

CONTACT: The Royal Society for the Protection of Birds, The Lodge, Sandy, Bedfordshire SG19 2DL; Royal Society for Nature Conservation, The Green, Witham Park, Waterside South, Lincoln LN5 7JR; 01767 68055

SALARY: From £12,000 to around £20,000 per annum (RSPB)

SKILLS: Able to identify wildlife, talk to visitors, work long hours

It is nature in the raw down at the bird reserve, with marauding badgers, foxes, crows, stray dogs and human egg-collectors fanatic enough to risk their lives to steal a rare egg. The trusty warden, armed with binoculars, mounts a 24-hour watch against these villains during the breeding season. Busiest times are from April to September, and that is when the majority of voluntary and seasonal wardens are recruited (details of summer contract posts on reserves from the RSPB).

There are thousands of applications from naturalists keen enough on conservation to spend their holidays in basic accommodation, unpaid, with no food provided, helping out on the reserves. As well as guarding nests, they keep records, maintain the habitat and escort visitors. You can be a voluntary warden from the age of 16, and the experience is useful in applying to be a summer warden (from age 20). The next step, as assistant warden, is a permanent job and leads on to Reserve Warden – but these permanent jobs are few and far between, almost as rare as eagles' eggs. The RSPB expects A-level qualifications, with biology/zoology favoured; some wardens are graduates.

Even on bird reserves, the warden, who is in charge of preserving the whole habitat, needs to be an all-round naturalist, interested in the flora as well as the fauna within its area. Thinning scrub, cutting reeds, cleaning ditches and beaches, and weeding islands, plus the maintenance of fencing and the building and repairing of hides, are jobs that continue into the winter time.

In summer, a large proportion of the fauna consists of the visitors, who will need guidance through the reserve, and answers to their questions, so the enjoyment of meeting people is all part of the job. Also important are organising surveys, collecting and collating the information brought in, keeping up records, encouraging the existing animals and birds to remain, and attracting more to the site. The warden has a very varied job that involves long hours - the hours of daylight - and is much in demand. However, with the cut-back in land use for farming, and the growth of interest in nature reserves and numbers of SSSIs (Site of Special Scientific Interest), the species Nature Reserve Warden could become less rare in the future.

Ocularist

CONTACT: The National Artificial Eye Service, 221 Bristol Avenue, Blackpool, Lancashire FY2 0BF; 01253 306467

SALARY: No fixed rate

SKILLS: Qualification as dispensing optician, dental technician or no special qualification. Good colour vision, manual dexterity, counselling skills

An ocularist (an American word) is someone who makes and fits artificial eyes. In fact, there are only about a dozen people in the country who do both making and fitting, and they are mainly qualified as dispensing opticians (responsible for supplying and fitting spectacles).

Training mainly comes from working with an experienced ocularist, self-taught experience (in making the eyes) or from working with the Department of Health, either as a technician making the eyes, or as a fitter.

Eyes used to be made in glass by the Viennese, who did very intricate work, but the skill has died out because the modern ones are made in acrylic, which can be moulded to the complexities of the socket and eye muscles, and will move. Also, they do not shatter if dropped. Advances in ophthalmic surgery in recent years have meant that a damaged eye can be repaired, rather than needing to be removed. Altogether there are only around 40,000 artificial eyes in the country, so it is pretty unlikely that you know anyone who has one.

It can take about three days to make an eye, and the artistic bit, the painting of the iris, when done by an ocularist specifically for a patient, is colour-matched against a photograph or drawn reference, then finished with a final coat of acrylic; eyes from manufacturers are chosen by the optician from a tray of samples, looking rather like a button card.

In the Department of Health the National Artificial Eye Service is administered by the Blackpool Wyre and Fylde

Community Health Services NHS Trust and has over 40,000 patients registered. Within the NAES the roles of orbital prosthetist (fitter) and ocular technician are separate and require different skills.

The orbital prosthetists are based at 16 NAES centres throughout England and are the people who see the patient in clinic, fit a temporary artificial eye, take an impression of the eye socket, make a wax mould and take a note of the colour and size of the iris, then send the details off to the NAES laboratory at Blackpool to be made by an ocular technician. The artificial eye is then sent back and the prosthetist fits and adjusts it if necessary (acrylic material can be easily adjusted to shape, and even re-polished if scratched). Then the patient returns each year to have the eye checked and polished. Obviously, the experience of having a new eye can be very traumatic for patients, especially if they have suffered a serious accident or cancer, and so the fitter must be able to care sympathetically for people who have suffered severe shock of this kind. Training in all areas of the work covers artificial eyes, cosmetic shells and facial prostheses and includes counselling skills. It takes between three and four years, first at the training school in Blackpool and then at one of the 16 centres. Salaries are from £10,573 to £16,278.

The ocular technicians who make the eyes may be given on-the-job training by one of the very few factories making artificial eyes, or by the Department of Health, in the training laboratory at Blackpool, which takes about two years. They may often have begun as dental technicians, as the type of materials and experience used are very much the same as in making false teeth and gums. In some hospital units, the technicians may also be making other prostheses (artificial parts of the body), such as eyelids, ears and cheeks. Some artistic skills are needed, for shaping and colouring the eyes, with an aptitude for adapting the technical training into an ability for making other things. Artificial eye technicians earn between £10,573 and £13,379.

Pastry Cook

CONTACT: National Association of Master Bakers,
            21 Baldock Street, Ware, Hertfordshire SG12 9DH;
            01920 468061

SALARY: Around £200 for a 39-hour week in small bakery;
            rates are higher in London where there is a shortage
            of skilled staff

SKILLS: Must be able to get up for early-morning start; phys-
            ical stamina; high standard of personal hygiene;
            good communication skills and ability to work in a
            team

One of the special treats of a visit to France or Austria is choosing which gateau slice to try: chocolate, mocha coffee, marron. Or rich choux pastries, oozing with cream; crisply delicious little *tartes*, filled with fresh strawberries, apple slices, blackcurrants or grapes piled on to a bed of pastry cream; petits fours; apple strudels, Danish pastries, rich with apricots, almonds, praline and icing. Then it is brought to you to eat with your freshly made real coffee, or you take it away to enjoy with your picnic lunch. There are not so many pastry and coffee shops in this country as on the continent, but they are popular in the tourist spots here.

Pastry cooks work not only in small businesses, such as bakeries and coffee shops, but also in large hotels, cruise ships and the armed services. Their work is really known as flour confectionery, and includes sweet and savoury pastries, cakes, biscuits and buns, plus the art of decoration. What we normally think of as confectionery – sweets and chocolates – is another side of the business.

Working with pastry includes the making of meat pies: steak and onion, steak and kidney, Cornish pasties, sausage rolls, chicken and mushroom, etc, using puff pastry or wholemeal pastry. Of course, a large proportion of the meat pies normally bought are made in factories, where the work is mainly done by machine. Even in a small shop, many of the goods sold may have been bought in frozen form, then cooked and, in the case of pastries, finished off with glazes, icing and cream, so that they are 'freshly baked' before sale. Quite a lot of these frozen pastries are imported from Belgium and Holland. Even custard tarts may be bought ready prepared and frozen. But the local bread shop, selling both new bread and pastries made on the premises, will make everything itself.

Here, the baker and pastry cook work together. The pastry cook has an advantage, as pastry can be prepared the night before, refrigerated overnight and baked the next day for sale in the morning; the baker, however, must start the bread making in the small hours of the morning, at around 2 am. In small bakeries, the pastry cook will help with the bread in the mornings and then go on to do the pastries.

Courses in basic bakery are run on both a full- and part-time basis at colleges and lead to an NVQ. The NVQs in Craft Bakery are offered by City and Guilds or Hotel and Catering Training Company (HCTC). They may be combined with apprenticeship at a bakery and on-the-job training. There are also further courses in the Design and Decoration of Flour Confectionery. This type of work could be taken up by mature adults; the National Association of Master Bakers has schemes to help those who decide they would like to set up on their own.

Piano Tuner

CONTACT: Pianoforte Tuners' Association, c/o 10 Reculver
Road, Herne Bay, Kent CT6 6LD; 01227 368808
(*send sae*)

EARNINGS: £28.50 to £30 per tuning session

SKILLS: Musical sense, but not necessary to be a pianist;
acute hearing; patience; social skills

One of the most irritating sounds on earth, not dissimilar to Chinese water torture, is the chink, chink, chink of a piano being tuned. When the tuner arrives everyone else tends to vacate the premises, to lurk out of earshot for an hour or so until the job is over. The piano tuner, of course, has to be able to stand it for life, but does have the pleasure of ending each session with a musical flourish to check the newly tuned instrument. Any pieces are suitable: jazz, pop or Bach. And those who have never had piano lessons can simply learn a couple of melodies by heart.

Singing or violin experience is in fact more valuable than playing the piano because tuning has more to do with getting exactly the right note out of each piano string, listening to the harmonic beats as the string is tightened.

A piano, once the casing is off, is like a harp lying on its side; each of the notes depressed by the pianist hits up to three strings, depending on the register, and each of these must be correctly tuned. As with other stringed instruments – guitars, violins, double basses, etc – the strings go out of tune, affected by heat and damp, as well as by use. The piano tuner travels around with a bag of tools including a tuning fork with which he tunes the A note, and spanners to tighten all the strings, regulating their notes against the A. It also contains spare strings, leather, felt pads, lead for the counterbalance weights and screwdrivers, for the tuner checks the instruments over as well as tuning them, and carries out any necessary maintenance and repairs that need to be done. Getting a concert grand ready for an evening performance could take half a day.

Both school leavers and mature people can take up this work. Training, which used to be by five-year apprenticeship in a piano factory, is now by college course; this gives less tuning experience than the old apprenticeship, but more technical training. College courses lead to City and Guilds certificates, or college certificates.

Two-year courses are held at the London Guildhall University and City of Leeds College of Music. Three-year courses are held at Newark and Sherwood College, Friary Road, Newark, Nottinghamshire NG24 1PB; the Royal National College for the Blind (which also takes sighted students), College Road, Hereford and Stevenson College of Further Education, Bankhead Avenue, Edinburgh EH11 4DE.

After their training, piano tuners work in piano factories, for piano dealers or other tuners. They must gain at least two years' experience before they can apply to join the Pianoforte Tuners' Association, which involves passing a test. Working for a dealer or tuner takes you into people's homes, so it is important to be able to get on well with customers. In rural areas this can involve a great deal of travelling between pianos, so it is normally necessary to be able to drive a car (blind or partially sighted tuners are usually ferried around by the customers). Tuners reckon that four pianos must be tuned per day to make the work economically viable. Normally a tuner can manage five a day. £23.93 to £39.89 per session is the charge recommended by the Association, though charges are often lower in rural areas, highest in London.

Picture Restorer

CONTACT: Association of British Picture Restorers,
Station Avenue, Kew, Surrey TW9 3QA;
0181 948 5644

SALARY: From £8000 per annum

SKILLS: No special art skills needed; good manual dexterity;
normal colour vision

It is reckoned that about 95 per cent of the people working as picture restorers are academically untrained – they simply fancy the idea and pick it up as they go along, though they may apprentice themselves to a recognised restorer (the Association has a list of members and is keen on raising standards). The hope is that any damage done by bad restoration is on bad pictures only and will be made good by a better job at some other time; the art trade is very circular and pictures keep coming round on to the market again.

Work is done mainly for dealers, and also for private collectors. Museums and galleries have their own staff who will have done postgraduate courses. The pinnacle is to work at the National Gallery, the Metropolitan Museum of Art in New York, or the Uffizi in Florence, employed as a civil servant. Salaries range from £8000 to £22,000, depending on age and experience.

At museum level, there's plenty of time to spend on conservation and the work is specialised and scientifically orientated. In the private sector, dealers may want a painting returned to them in only a month. Restorers working for dealers may earn very little, but some run companies specialising in the work. Much is done by the dealers themselves.

Some restorers specialise in paper, restoring books, manuscripts and watercolours; others in oil paintings. They clean the painting, removing surface dirt, smoke deposits and fly spots. If necessary, they clean off the old varnish and discoloured old restorations, and paste in or touch in flaking or missing paint and apply a protective coat of varnish. Any holes or tears in the canvas are filled in and weak or torn canvases are re-lined (a new canvas is glued to the back to reinforce the old one), and distorted canvases are re-tensioned. Different problems have to be solved when the painting is a mural, or done on a wooden panel – with cracks, warps and woodworm. Some of the works of art could be as old as fourteenth century, some less than 50 years old. Restorers are often asked for opinions on the authenticity or age of a painting.

Courses are held at the Courtauld Institute of Art, Somerset House, Strand, London WC2; University of Northumbria at Newcastle, Burt Hall, Newcastle upon Tyne NE1 8ST; and the Hamilton Kerr Institute, Whittlesford, Cambridge. Entry is at postgraduate level; degree subjects are normally Fine Arts, History of Art or a science, such as physics or chemistry. Those with an arts degree should have O-level/GCSE Science or A-level Chemistry. There are courses in the USA and Europe as well – but competition for entry to all courses is fierce. The three-year full-time Courtauld course, for instance, takes only five students each year.

Salaries in the museums and galleries follow appropriate civil service grades, whereas in the private sector they will vary widely depending on experience and competence. Entry salaries in the civil service tend to be higher than the private sector, but at the top of the profession larger salaries can be earned as a private restorer – £50,000 plus. Civil service rates are higher in London, from around £16,000; top rates are £39,360 to £57,600 (in London).

Puppeteer

CONTACT: The Puppet Centre, BAC,
166 Lavender Hill, London SW11 5TN;
0171 228 5335 (Please enclose sae)

SALARY: From £200 per week

SKILLS: Craft and creative skills; interest in puppets

Puppets are not only found at the end of the pier these days, or even in the shopping arcade or school classroom. Switch on the television, and you will see them in advertisements, children's programmes and satirical programmes – of which *Spitting Image* is an outstanding example. *The Tube, Rainbow, The Muppets* (of course) and even *ET* (where puppetry was used to mock up the bicycle flight) have also made puppets into screen stars.

Some of the puppets are made by puppet makers for use in stage productions, television, film and advertising; most are made by the puppeteers themselves. They use a variety of materials, including wood, celastic, polystyrene, plastic wood, papier mâché, latex, foam and soft materials. Some are glove puppets, like the traditional Punch and Judy, others are operated by strings attached to overhead rods (the marionettes) and others by rods either attached to the head or operated from below. There are also shadow or silhouette puppets, in which the images are projected on to a screen. Some are huge, made for street performances, or processions.

Wooden puppets, such as a traditional-looking Punch, call for skills in woodcarving (and sewing) and could take as long as three months to make. Being a puppeteer calls for a wide range of theatrical skills, including writing the material, making the booth and scenery, arranging lighting, sound systems, and taping a musical accompaniment, plus manipulating, performing (all those voices) and changing scenery during the performance. Puppeteers may work solo, or in companies of three or four members.

Some puppet shows are given in theatres (the Little Angel Marionette Theatre in Islington is a famous one and sometimes offers apprenticeships to aspiring puppeteers); others are performed outdoors, in local halls, schools and for private functions such as birthday parties. Valuable use can be made of puppets in education, not only in classrooms in this country, but also to help teach primary health care in developing countries.

Toy-making courses, such as the part-time course at the London Guildhall University, include puppet making, and the Puppet Centre can give information about other courses and workshops.

The London School of Puppetry, 2 Legard Road, London N5 1DE (0171 359 7357) runs courses in performance skills including puppet manipulation, employment opportunities and working with artists from other artforms. As well as one-day courses, there is a modular course (£1456) and a one-year part-time course (£1800). There is also an Advanced Diploma in Puppetry offered by the Central School of Speech and Drama, Embassy Theatre, 64 Eton Avenue, London NW3 3HY and Nottingham Trent University offers puppetry modules as part of a Theatre Design Degree. There may be a chance to study puppetry as part of a modular course in performing arts, theatre design or design at a drama school or university.

Puppeteers develop their own characters, though there are still many (known as 'professors') who work with Mr Punch. There is an international flavour to puppetry, with performers visiting the USA, Canada and the Middle East as well as Europe, and puppeteers from countries with a long tradition of the art, including the Far East, France, Italy, Germany, Czechoslovakia and Hungary, visiting the UK.

The Puppet Centre has a Directory of Professional Puppeteers and information about puppet theatres and collections, and notes on training opportunities, as well as a book list and its own magazine, *Animations.*

Race Track Marshal

CONTACT: British Motor Racing Marshals Club, 2 Temple Close, Bletchley, Milton Keynes MK3 7RG; 01908 378750

SALARY: None

SKILLS: Enthusiasm for motor racing

If you are a keen spectator of motor racing, either within the din of the circuit itself, or from the peace of an armchair in front of the television, you will probably have envied the chaps in orange boiler suits who have managed to find themselves a wonderful job stewarding the races, and being able to watch them for nothing. In fact, you would have been wrong, because the people who turn out to help at race meetings do so voluntarily, for the most part. Only full-time employees of the motor clubs are paid. Scrutineers and timekeepers receive a nominal amount plus travel expenses, marshals (in the boiler suits) may be given a meal voucher and the stewards, who are concerned with rules and regulations, receive only expenses. Most race meetings are held at weekends or bank holidays.

At a club meeting there will be three stewards: one from the RAC (the governing body) and two nominated by the club, plus around 80 marshals and the rescue unit, crash crews and medical staff. There must be two ambulances and two doctors standing by, and a rescue unit with cutting and resuscitation equipment to deal with anyone trapped in their car. Motor racing includes sprinting and hill climbing as well as racing proper, and of course most circuits also have hot rod bangers, go-karts, motor-cycle racing and rally cross on Sundays all through the year.

On race days marshals are distributed round the track in groups of five or six at marshal points, situated every 300 to

400 yards and under the control of one observer; others are responsible for the paddock and the pit and there are also spectator, incident, fire and flag marshals.

They are given training sessions so that they know how to cope with an 'incident', using MOT write-offs to fake accidents. These are turned upside down with people inside as if injured or unconscious, and a rescue crew has to cut them out. Then the car is turned the other way up and set alight, and the trainees have to douse the fire.

Marshals are normally members of motor clubs; some may themselves drive at club level, others may never have driven on a race track, but wish they had. Certainly, they get a good view of the racing on the track side of the barriers.

Those with experience of club-level marshalling can go on to senior level: Formula One Grand Prix races (still unpaid); or train to become licensed rescue vehicle crew members; or they may work their way up. From standing at the side of the track with a fire extinguisher they may go on to waving a flag, then being official observer, then becoming a judge, and then clerk of the course, responsible for running the event on the day, and they may eventually have enough experience to make it to steward.

Stewards will have a keen interest in motor racing, and are often former competition drivers. They need to be able to understand all the practicalities involved in racing, and have a good knowledge of the rule book, which is quite a weighty document. They need to know where to look something up if there is a query; if there is a protest by a competitor, the stewards convene a meeting and then come to their decision.

It may not be a job, but it's a very responsible and full-time hobby.

Recruitment Consultant

CONTACT: The Institute of Employment Consultants, 6 Guildford Road, Woking, Surrey GU22 7PX; 01483 766442

EARNINGS: From £15,000 basic plus commission

SKILLS: Self-confidence; selling skills; good telephone
manner; ability to negotiate; prepared to work hard

In the job advertisement section of the newspapers there are
normally plenty of ads for 'telesales' staff – the people who
have to put up with short and snappy answers when they
phone to offer double-glazing or similar services. 'Cold calling'
– making calls to people who are not expecting sales talk from
a stranger when they pick up the phone – is a tough training
in developing a good telephone manner, taking disappoint-
ments (dozens every day) pleasantly and, eventually, negotiating a sale.

Those who stick at telesales and make a success of the job
will soon be directing a team of staff, on the way to becoming
a sales director.

The recruitment consultant is also selling – not products
but people, and their skills. In fields in which there is a severe
shortage of trained staff, such as computer work, salaries can
be high. The consultant working for an agency has the job of
finding companies who need the type of skills offered by
candidates. The companies pay commission (15 to 20 per
cent of the first year's salary) to the agency once a candidate
has been successfully placed.

The companies normally give an induction course and
further training to consultants in skills such as how to:
present a good image on the phone; cultivate a positive
attitude; negotiate salaries and terms of employment on
behalf of candidates; overcome negative attitudes – perhaps

on the part of employers who are not initially interested in taking on the extra staff suggested. There's also instruction on the guidelines laid down by the Department of Employment.

One agency group operates on American hard-sell lines. Staff are expected to stand up while phoning, so they project their voices, sound enthusiastic and not lazy – and keep at it, dialling another number as soon as each call is finished without replacing the phone. When they've arranged an interview for their candidate, they can sit down! However, most consultants can be more relaxed, though basic patterns of working are the same. They each build up their own databases of employers and candidates, using advertisements, referrals, annually published lists of companies and recommendations from people they have done business with in the past. Like any sales work, prime 'selling time' is 9 to 5.30, when it's easiest to reach people, but background work needs to be done outside those hours, and during weekends.

As consultants move up through the agency, taking charge of teams of staff, they can earn extra commission based on turnover. This type of recruitment consultancy is a young person's job; many are taken on at 18 but the agencies prefer graduates of under 25, with two years' commercial experience. Though an average income of basic salary plus commission would be around £20K to £35K (£20,000 to £35,000 – this is K country!) per year, basic salaries can rise to £20K plus commission, and it is possible for a 22-year-old to be earning as much as £100K or even more.

The highest earnings go to recruitment consultants who specialise in recruiting computer staff, but there are many other fields in which consultants (and agencies) specialise, such as nursing, banking, secretarial, accountancy and engineering. Eventually consultants move into executive selection, staying within their specialist area, dealing with senior staff in higher management jobs, and very often they eventually leave the agency to set up their own business.

Roof Tiler

CONTACT: Local building firms or Institute of Roofing,
            24 Weymouth Street, London W1N 3FA;
            0171 436 0103

SALARY: Around £70 per day, self-employed

SKILLS: Physical fitness, common sense, willingness to work
            out of doors and cope with cold in winter; no fear of
            heights!

If you'd have no hesitation in coping with a large lady on a
steeply sloping roof in the rain, then you've got what it takes
to be a roof tiler. You may encounter duchesses and coun-
tesses up there, too, as well as ordinary ladies, though
differently sized slates are normally identified by their measurements nowadays, instead of those old romantic names.
As well as slates, a roof slater and tiler works with clay,
concrete and asbestos tiles and with lead, zinc and sometimes
copper.

Very cold weather in the winter, gales and heavy rain can stop work, though once a stripped roof has been covered with felt and battening the tiling can be completed, even in wet conditions. In a large firm there is other work that can be done when the weather is very bad, but this can be more difficult for the self-employed tiler.

Many people who work on their own have had no formal training, having picked up the skills from other craftsmen, but to do this you must have your wits about you and be able to use your common sense, and take a pride in your work. There is the chance to specialise in the repair and restoration of beautiful old buildings, using old materials such as the handmade clay Kent peg tiles, salvaged from demolitions.

Self-employed tilers normally work with one partner, but in a large building firm they work either in pairs or in teams of up to six. Work may vary from new housing estates, sports halls, repairs to older properties or restorations of ancient buildings, including cathedrals. Training is organised through the Construction Industry Training Board's Youth Training programme and then continued apprenticeship with an approved firm, where trainees learn about various aspects of construction. During the first year, 13 to 24 weeks are spent at a college or training centre, combined with work on site.

The normal training period is three years; the CITB training counts towards an apprenticeship. Apprentices' pay starts at £74 per week at 16 (1994 rates) rising to £173 on passing a skills test. A roof slater and tiler may train altogether for five to ten years to a very high standard, starting off as a labourer apprentice and working up (literally). The more skills gained, and the more intricate the job, the higher the amount that can eventually be earned; wages are normally on a par with skilled bricklayers and carpenters. Often work is subcontracted for a lump sum payment, so the quicker the job is done, the more money can be made.

Tiling is an ideal job for those who don't mind hard work and fresh air, and who are strong enough to do the heavy work of stripping and re-covering a roof with felt, and humping the tiles or slates up the ladders. Once at the top there is the bonus of stupendous views that most people never see.

Sailmaker

CONTACT: Sailmaking factories; see yachting magazines or
            Association of British Sailmakers, 2 Orchard Road,
            Lock's Heath, Southampton SO3 6PR

SALARY: Trainee, £2 per hour; from £3.50 per hour when
            fully trained

SKILLS: Manual dexterity; a designer needs A-level Maths
            and Physics, technical drawing and computer skills

Yachting is another of those leisure sports that is growing in popularity and, like snooker, takes place in everyone's living room, via TV. Even those who feel sick at the sight of a gangplank have admired the speed and grace of the flying hulls and billowing spinnakers during Cowes Week races. Those who may not feel quite ready for the thrills and spills of the Americas Cup, or climbing the main mast of a tall sailing ship, still get a lot of fun out of dinghy sailing and windsurfing on reservoirs inland as well as round the coast.

Catering for this trade, sailmakers cope with anything, from the smallest dinghy mainsails to the huge racing spinnakers and laminate mainsails for the Americas Cup races, which can cost over £30,000, and a spinnaker over £12,000. Materials may be very lightweight nylon, up to heavyweight terylene. Most of the work is done by machine, although restoration work on an old boat whose owner insists on everything looking original could involve (expensive) hand sewing.

Experienced sailmakers design the sails for new boats, after talking to the boat's designer and spar maker, or advise on the type of sails that will be suitable in different climates – winds are heavier in our northern parts because they are laden with moisture; in the Mediterranean or on the Equator the velocity is the same but the weight is lighter.

Designing and making sails can take you back to the days of the old square riggers or to the extravagant modern designs of the parachute-like spinnakers, with colourful shapes that may be contrasting pieces of fabric let into the sail, or complicated patterns that are painted on like a child playing with a paintbox – or an ad man's wildest dreams.

Training schemes for sailmakers (men and women) are organised from time to time by the Association of British Sailmakers, but most sailmakers enter a sailmaker's 'loft' as school leavers and train on the job, moving round most of the aspects of sailmaking from cutting out to machining, hand finishing and 'rubbing down' (rubbing the sail into shape after the pieces have been joined up and machined together).

It takes four or five years to become fully trained, and most sailmakers stay in the same loft because the techniques used in each one are very individual, so it is difficult to move from one to another. Most sailmaking lofts are sited near the sea, and are part of the local sailing world.

The work includes making sailcover and spray hoods to protect the sails against rain, as well as repairs to split material that has perhaps been hauled in too tight by over-enthusiastic racing crews. The older-established companies usually specialise in the larger boats of 40 ft and more; smaller new companies work on the shorter lengths – and are sometimes known to sink after a season or two.

At present, with the popularity of sailing, sailmakers are in demand. Their busiest time is from January to October, and many lofts would not be able to operate without part-time workers, often mothers working while their children are at school. A machinist earns from £2.80 to £3.50 per hour when trained. A sailmaker/machinist, who is more experienced but not responsible for cutting, earns from £3.80 to £4.50. A bench hand will do cutting out, and earns £4.50 to £5. A top designer/cutter, working on the busy South coast, will earn around £5.50 per hour. Cutters now use laser plotters to draw out and cut the panels for sails; so computer skills are necessary as well as A-level maths and physics, which should include a knowledge of aerodynamics and hydrodynamics.

Shepherd

CONTACT: Your nearest college of agriculture or TEC

SALARY: Craft workers aged 20 plus, from £166.85 (1994)
            per week plus overtime, from £6.41 per hour (rates
            depend on qualifications)

SKILLS: Physical health, strength and stamina

Shepherds come into the news whenever there is a hard winter, or cold and wet early spring. It can be a very exhausting time for them, as they struggle to rescue flocks trapped in deep drifts, provide them with food, and rescue the lambs that seem to be born when conditions are worst, when it is pouring with rain.

The shepherds seen on television news at these times are often those on the hill farms, where the sheep are widely distributed. The farmers in these areas, including the Lake District, Scotland and North Wales, are normally small farmers, owning their farms and working them with little, if any, hired help. In the lowland areas, there are more mixed arable and livestock farms, which may be owned by large commercial organisations. Where sheep flocks are only one part of the work of the farm, a shepherd may be expected to do general work at times of the year when the sheep are less demanding.

Like other types of farm work, being a shepherd means going out in all weathers, and being alone a great deal of the time. Feeding the flock during the winter is followed by the lambing season. The ewes may be brought under cover for a short time for lambing, but are then turned out into the open fields as soon as possible, to help prevent the spread of disease and to save space and labour.

Sick lambs, or those that have lost their mothers, may have to be brought into the kitchen as 'sock' lambs to be fed until their strength is built up enough for them to be returned to their mothers. Sometimes orphan lambs can be fostered on to another ewe (a difficult procedure that involves wrapping the orphan in the skin of the ewe's own dead lamb). Returning the sock lambs to the flock is essential; a sweet little baby lamb frisking in the kitchen can become a remarkably over-pampered, bullying old sheep in the back garden a few months later.

The shepherd has a round-the-clock duty at lambing time, overseeing normal births, helping with the difficult ones, as well as feeding etc.

During the summer the shepherd is responsible for dipping the sheep to protect them against parasites, worming and vaccinating them and changing their pastures. Though the shepherd may also become involved in shearing, the job is often done by jolly gangs of New Zealand shearers who do the work at lightning speed on a contract basis, moving around the country. The sheep need to be checked constantly for signs of disease and disability. (Sheep are very prone to foot problems and there nearly always seems to be at least one in a flock which is lame!) Towards the autumn lambs have to be graded and sorted for selling and the older ewes removed and replaced with young stock. After the rams have been put in with the flock in autumn there is an extra responsibility to protect the pregnant ewes and give them properly balanced feed so that healthy lambs will be born the following spring.

Throughout all this work, of course, the shepherd is helped by one or two trusty collies – or, increasingly, by zappy little three-wheeled buggies or trail bikes that help the shepherd cut groups of sheep out of the flock as they are needed.

The ATB-Landbase programme can combine on-the-job training with college courses, leading to NVQ or National Certificate qualifications that can bring wages at a higher level. The wider the training in agriculture, the better, especially if it includes the use and maintenance of farm machinery.

Snooker Player

CONTACT: The World Professional Billiards & Snooker Association Ltd, 27 Oakfield Road, Clifton, Bristol BS8 2AT; 0117 9744491

EARNINGS: From nothing to £1m!

SKILLS: Natural ability to play any type of ball game

Snooker is a popular sport throughout the world, with its interests spreading via direct-relay overseas broadcasts and sky channels to Australia and the Far East as well as Europe. Belgium is one of the countries that has recently taken it up as a popular activity, with the result that British coaches can work in the Belgian clubs for two or three days a week all the year round.

With the world championship winner being awarded around £190,000 in prize money, the top players could earn mega-figures of £¼ million to £1 million in a year, plus the other benefits of sponsorships, and syndicate rights, which means attaching their name to billiard cues or tables as well as doing exhibition matches.

Entry to the top ranks of snooker was until recently very strictly controlled, with only 128 players able to compete in professional events worldwide. Now the rules of the World Professional Billiard and Snooker Association (WPBSA) have been changed, so that anyone who is over the age of 16 on September 30 can write to the WPBSA for a membership application form and join on payment of an initial £587.50 fee; the annual membership fee will be around £117.50.

Other costs are liable to be high: paying entry fees to all the UK tournaments would cost around £1000; entering major ranking tournaments throughout the world could come to £2100 plus travel, food and accommodation. It could cost altogether £15,000 per year to play in major tournaments. Big tournaments in Hong Kong and Australia offer prize money totalling around £¼m, but there are more competitors, from countries such as Singapore, Hong Kong and Canada, going after the top prizes. A snooker player needs to be both good and lucky to win – the day of a major tournament is no time to have an 'off day'.

Young players have been known to start their careers in the back rooms of pubs, but since pubs rarely have space for a full-size snooker table, most beginners learn the game in snooker centres.

Those who show promise may be taken on to work in a snooker centre or club and given training by the management; if they show talent they may be sponsored by the management or an agent and entered in junior tournaments, local leagues, county and eventually national and international competitions. The manager or agent would pay their expenses, and take a percentage of any prize money.

The WPBSA runs a training scheme for professional players who want to become coaches. The scheme leads to examinations for registration with the WPBSA as a qualified coach.

Those who do not make a good living from winning tournaments (only around 30 players in the world can do so) can work as a 'professional' in a club, or as a coach. The snooker season runs from 1 September to the World Championship at the end of April, but during the summer players can work as coaches in holiday camps or clubs, or go overseas, to those Hong Kong and Australian tournaments, for instance. It is a lucrative market for good players.

With new snooker centres now in most largish towns, there are opportunities for a growing number of young players. It helps, of course, to have a natural talent for games like tennis and golf and the kind of personality to develop an entertaining style for those exhibition matches at which the top players dazzle with their expertise.

Sound Recordist

CONTACT: Television and film companies

EARNINGS: BBC Trainee, £12,000 to £14,500; £120 to £250 per
               day after training

SKILLS: GCE O-level/GCSE Maths and Physics; a
               commitment to sound (sound for school plays,
               hospital radio); very good hearing

The sound recordist is the member of the sound team who gets out and about on location, whereas the sound engineer works in the studio, playing about with mixing decks. A third member is the specialist music engineer, who is responsible for the recording of concerts, and for records made in the studio.

A lot of the work is done for television and film, rather than radio. A radio reporter going out to get a story takes his or her own tape recorder and microphone along, but a television news or current affairs team consists of reporter plus sound recordist, camera operator and an assistant who acts as boom operator and holds the microphone. Working with film means fitting the sound to the picture.

Being with a film crew on location is the glamorous side – hanging a radio mike on to famous stars, sitting up in a tree swinging a microphone as a scene is acted below. It can also involve long hours of excruciating boredom waiting for shots to be set up; worst are television commercials that may take from 8.30 am to 10 pm for a 30-second end product. Weather and the time of year affect drama work. Although rain does not put a stop to TV news and current affairs, good weather is needed for drama, as well as long daylight hours for filming, so January and February tend to be quiet times.

The documentary sphere is more involved with reality, and

can lead to exciting and rewarding work, overseas as well as in the UK – in China or the Antarctic, in Eastern Europe, or crossing the Sahara desert.

Those who work on a freelance basis do not get as many chances for these trips abroad as permanent staff employed by the television companies, such as the BBC, who use their own people before bringing in freelances.

Sound recordists belong to BECTU (Broadcasting Entertainment Cinematograph & Theatre Union), which insists on applicants having a job before applying to join. Many sound recordists have begun in the film business as a 'gofer' and picked up their training on the job. The BBC's training programme, which gives all-round training, is accepted as being the best in the world. Many freelances and ITV sound technicians have had BBC training. But there are very few openings, and as more independent production companies are used for making TV films, the numbers of BBC staff have shrunk. After training, technicians are paid individually according to grades negotiated with BECTU. Lowest are the rates for documentaries and short films such as in-house training videos; better are rates for feature films, and best are those in the commercial sector, such as films for advertising.

The BBC training involves three years' technical training combined with on-the-job learning, after which the trainee is at basic technical operator grade, working on simple locations, public address equipment or laying out microphones for an orchestra under supervision (in a film group, the technician would be an assistant film recordist at this stage). Promotion to recordist is slow (at least ten years) but then come the exciting opportunities of perhaps doing a 90-minute play on film, immediately followed by a stereo Omnibus Special or a contribution to a David Attenborough wildlife series.

While a sound engineer must be the type to work late into the night in the dark in the dubbing theatre to get the right results, a location recordist must be resourceful, understand production requirements and be prepared to function half-way up a Chilean mountain while being eaten by a goat, and have enough political sophistication to record an interview with rebels without getting shot or upsetting the interviewees.

Spy

CONTACT: Wait to be asked

SALARY: Civil service rates

SKILLS   Languages or science; ability to lead two separate lives; must be willing to undertake positive vetting and a lie detector test

There are spies and spies; some get sucked into the business through greed, blackmail, fear, affairs with people who turn out to be another country's agents, or because they bear a grudge against their employers (there are industrial spies as well). Others are recruited as university graduates, members of the armed forces, diplomats or members of other government services. Trade delegates and journalists may do the odd bit of spying, too.

Spy satellites and aircraft that can photograph movements and buildings far below do a lot of the intelligence-gathering nowadays, directed by agents on the ground. That intelligence has to be evaluated and shared with the CIA and other agencies.

CIA recruitment literature describes the job as having 'less to do with cloaks and daggers than with painstaking, generally tedious collection of facts, analysis of facts and quick clear evaluation'. So the old-fashioned masters of disguise are out – too easily detected in today's bureaucratic world – and it is trade delegations who may be bristling with miniature cameras and microdot film, who meet the contact and make a 'drop'.

Spies abroad are handled by MI6, the Secret Intelligence Service, and the bulk of their activities involves the painstaking and often boring gathering of information about drugs, terrorism and arms proliferation, not only in the Middle East, but Eastern Europe and other countries as well – languages are needed for this work.

The other branch of the intelligence service is MI5, responsible for intelligence operations and for counter-espionage – rooting out agents that have been recruited or planted in this country to send information out.

For those who prefer spying from a distance, there is GCHQ (Government Communications Headquarters) at Cheltenham, where code and cipher breakers work on signals intercepted all over the world, and search for whispers of new weapons, military movements, suspicious diplomatic activity. In this field of electronic espionage, prosaic computer analysts evaluate the stored information.

The police have their spies, too – in Special Branch, whose role is to foil terrorism, often working with MI5.

Spying might seem like a murky business – but it was successful in stopping the invasion of America by Soviet weapons secreted into Cuba. It might have prevented the Falklands conflict had there been more agents at the time in Argentina – and influenced the invasion of Kuwait by Iraq if the top brass had believed the information their spy satellites were giving them.

Stately Home Guide

CONTACT: Local stately home (in Yellow Pages)

EARNINGS: From £3.50 per hour

SKILLS: Should enjoy and be used to dealing with the public;
               interest in the particular property; good
               appearance and speaking voice

There is something very pleasant about the thought of sitting in a beautiful room, surrounded by valuable objects and drinking in the historical atmosphere of a stately home all day as a job. Unfortunately, the rapturous communion with timeless beauty is liable to be shattered by nine coachloads of tourists, including parties of French school children, by little boys who are sick on the carpet in the middle of a bank holiday when the place is packed, or who feel an urgent need to visit the loo at the furthest point from the plumbing. Or there may be a minor emergency, such as an old lady falling down the marble staircase and breaking her leg, or even a fire.

This is why someone who 'loves working with beautiful things' and is 'so interested in history' may be less likely to get taken on at the interview than the ex-publican, barmaid or shop assistant who is used to coping with the public, from primary school children to visitors in their eighties. Staff in stately homes would be expected to bone up about the history of the building and the objects in it, and, of course, to have a genuine interest in the building and its period.

Some of these tourist attractions are run privately such as Blenheim, Longleat or Penshurst Place in Kent, others are run by the National Trust or English Heritage. In houses with suites of rooms leading into each other, such as Blenheim and Chartwell, visitors are taken round by guided tour only; in others the visitors wander round freely, with guided tours offered as special arrangements. Both types of organisation employ more 'room watchers' or stewards than guides. These people keep an eye on a couple of rooms or a complete floor and are expected to be able to answer questions on the rooms. Both room stewards, who may sometimes act as guides, or guides themselves, need to be outgoing people who are not afraid to go up to visitors and offer help, or have the tact to leave them to wander around alone. In this way they have the chance to meet many people from overseas as well as from all over Britain, who are likely to share a common interest.

Guides must be willing to read a great deal so that they can answer all sorts of questions about the objects in the rooms, the life of the present or past owners and the history not only of the building but also its period. No guesswork is allowed during a guided tour, no notes – and no unnecessary rattling on, either. A good speaking voice is one that carries to all members of the group (usually about 15) of eager visitors; languages, such as French and German, are an advantage.

A room steward earns £3.50 to £4.50 per hour. A guide, taking a group of visitors round the building, earns from £7 to £15 per tour – which would take an hour, but involve up to two hours in the building. The rate for a tour in a foreign language would be higher, especially if the guide can speak Japanese.

The work is seasonal, and usually part time. National Trust room stewards are often members of the Trust, willing to give their time voluntarily, and may work only two days in a season. Rates paid to their guides vary according to the properties. Other guides work two or three days a week, and of course must be prepared to work weekends and bank holidays. Ages range from 30 to 70, with many housewives and retired people enjoying an outside interest. Students may be taken on to do surveys, or help with the catering or souvenir shop – good experience for an interesting job later.

Steeplejack

CONTACT: National Federation of Master Steeplejacks and Lightning Conductor Engineers, 6th Floor, Epic House, Charles Street, Leicester LE1 3SH; 0116 2538915

SALARY: £217.83 minimum weekly rate (advanced steeple-jack) (1994)

SKILLS: Good head for heights – maybe 280 metres

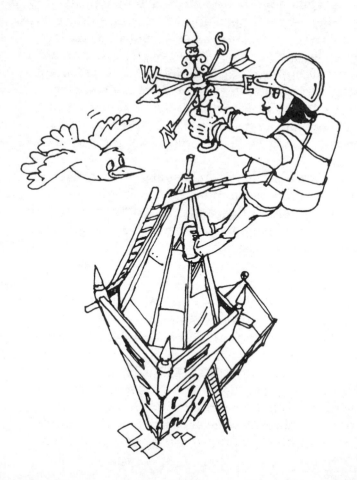

Steeplejacks are a somewhat maverick group within the building trade, for their proud boast is that they can tackle any job, at any height and in any trade. Normally construction work is strictly demarcated, but none of the ordinary trades are too keen to do their work swinging in space in a bosun's seat, way above the heads of ordinary mortals.

Once steeplejacks relied on a kite to carry the rope up to the top of a factory chimney or other tall structure; now they are more likely to use extendable timber or aluminium ladders fixed progressively to the structure, followed by complex modular scaffolds at the top.

When in position, the steeplejack is mostly employed on repair and maintenance work, painting, pointing brickwork and masonry. Basic electrical skills are needed for some jobs.

Many steeplejack firms specialise; some deal exclusively with erecting and maintaining lightning conductors, others with aluminium-clad chimneys, power station chimneys, or demolition work. One firm has worked on early-warning antennae for the USA, another, more traditionally, with flagstaffs. Also traditional: restoration of church spires and towers, and monuments – including Nelson's Column.

Training is carried out by the Construction Industry Training Board for the Steeplejack Industry Training Group Association. There are NVQs at levels 2 and 3, as well as skill testing. Many people enter the industry through a Youth Training programme. The CITB's Civil Engineering College at Bircham Newton Training Centre, Kings Lynn, Norfolk includes a steeplejack course. The course is combined with work experience; it aims 'to develop a sense of responsibility, character and leadership potential, not only as an individual but more important as a member of a team'. The courses, for those aged 16 and over, are an entry to the steeplejack industry's own apprenticeship scheme.

During the first year, the courses cover induction, basic rigging, laddering and means of access, scaffolding, brick-work pointing and repairs, painting and chimney banding and lightning conductor theory. The second year includes rigging, steel chimneys, rendering repairs, basic photography, reporting, abrasive wheels, cutting and welding. So, if you want to be on top of the world – here's your chance.

Stone Mason

CONTACT: Careers Advisory Service, Construction Industry Training Board, Bircham Newton, King's Lynn, Norfolk PE3 6RH; 01553 776677 (ext 2466)

SALARY: Minimum £4.19 per hour (average £6 per hour); minimum rate for qualified craftsmen, £163.41 per week

SKILLS: Physical strength; prepared to work out of doors; manual dexterity

Stone masonry is the oldest of the arts, or crafts, going back to Egyptian times, when the tools were made of bronze. The Assyrians took toolmaking a step further, using iron to make their chisels sharper and harder-wearing. Stone masons and sculptors still use the same type of traditional hand tools today, though since those times there has been another labour-saving advance - powered tools. The tombstones made by monumental masons are done by machine.

With the repair and restoration of old buildings, especially cathedrals and churches that are showing the wear of centuries, becoming an important task, stone masons can be involved in skilled and very satisfying work. There are two types of mason employed in the building trade: banker masons and fixer masons. The banker mason cuts and shapes stones using both the old hand tools, hammer and chisels - and powered tools. The stones may be square or shaped blocks, or carved into the classic leaf and lattice patterns, or even into figures and faces. Fixer masons are responsible for fixing the stones on site by laying them with mortar. Often this can involve coping with very large and heavy stones that have to be lifted into place using special equipment.

Decorative stone carving is very advanced work that is also done by sculptors, though stone masons may be used rather than sculptors for reasons of economy. Restoration work may be carried out for organisations such as the National Trust, local authorities, for civic buildings such as town halls and private clients. The work can involve a great deal of travelling around the country.

Someone who has artistic abilities, and may even have done an art school training, can become apprenticed to a stone mason working on his own, and learn about working in the various types of stone and the skills and techniques of carving. Sculptors working in stone may do restoration work, special commissions for clients, or freestyle work for sale, such as garden statuary or fountains. It may mean sweeping out the studio and making the tea to start with, but will eventually lead to the 'great adventure' – of carving into those pristine blocks of stone.

The training scheme organised by the Construction Industry Training Board involves a three-year period of work in the industry combined with training at a college or training centre. A list of firms that work in stone carving, repair and restoration is available from the Stone Federation, 82 New Cavendish Street, London W1M 8AD.

Stunt Performer

CONTACT: British Actors Equity Association, Guild House, Upper St Martins Lane, London WC2H 9EG; 0171 379 6000

EARNINGS: Stunt performer, £313 per day, £1251 per week; stunt arranger £397.50 per day, £1590 per week

SKILLS: Acting ability and membership of Equity; six qualifications in fighting (fencing, juko, aikido, wrestling, other martial arts, boxing); falling (trampolining, diving, parachuting); riding and driving (horses, cars, motor-cycles); agility and strength (gymnastics); water (swimming, sub-aqua); miscellaneous (ie ballet/athletic dance); age 18 or over; not more than 30. Personality: cool but not fearless

There's something about the idea of falling 50 feet out of a second-floor window, gun in hand and with clothes on fire, that attracts youngsters from six years old to 50, so every time a James Bond film is shown on television, there is a flood of enquiries to Equity, the actors' union, from would-be stunt performers.

It is not a job for the bold gung-ho type, who is careless of safety and could kill not only himself but someone else as well through not taking proper precautions. The skill lies in knowing how to avoid danger; even falling off a chair is less likely to lead to injury if it is done by a stunt performer who is trained to take knocks and falls, and who keeps in practice by making regular contact with the judo mat.

Stunt performers rig their own jumps and car crashes, using crash pads and special equipment, and working with a technician they know they can trust. On a film there may be various skills called for such as riding over fences, crashing a car or an 80ft fall. The stunt arranger chooses stunt performers experienced in each of the special skills needed. It can mean working on films all over the world – in America, Canada, the Philippines, even China. Top actors have their own stunt doubles, who must be able to act well enough to look convincing as the star. Although the actors may think they are as good at hell-for-leather riding as anyone else, the producer will not want to chance a broken limb, and insist on a double for the risky bits.

A stunt arranger working for a TV film will earn almost £400 a day, and a stunt performer over £300, but there is no guarantee of continuous work. A stunt performer may get the chance to work only twice a year – hardly enough to pay the insurance bills. There is also the cost of special equipment, such as a fire suit like those worn by Formula One racing drivers, for a job that involves being engulfed in flames, or wet suit for hours spent under water. So most stunt performers have another job.

With so much care taken over safety, it takes some time to get on to the Register of Stunt Performers and Arrangers as a full member. First comes probationary membership, which means working only under the charge of a full member of the register; after three years as a probationary member there is an assessment of your work record and it is decided whether intermediate status can be granted. This means being able to go out and take a risk with yourself only, with the chance to work for BBC, ITV and film companies as a stunt performer as long as actors and other stunt performers are not working with you and involved in the risk. After two years the stunt performer can apply for full membership of the register, which means being able to arrange stunts for actors and other stunt performers. It can take 20 years to become a topline stunt arranger; tricks of the trade are passed on by others: how to do a saddle fall, how to fall out of a window, how to break a window without being speared, how to prepare a vehicle for a spectacular crash. As easy as falling off a log?

Tattoo Artist

CONTACT: Association of Professional Tattoo Artists (APTA),
            118 Shirley Road, Southampton;
            British Tattoo Artists Federation, 389 Cowley Road,
            Oxford OX4 2BS

EARNINGS: Sessions are priced at £35 to £60 (in London) per
            hour

SKILLS: Artistic ability; steady hands

The most famous tattoo, said to have been sported by many
an admiral, is the one of a hunt in full cry down the subject's
back, with the fox disappearing down ... well, disappearing.
But, of course, it is not only admirals who are embellished
with decoration; there are as many women customers as men,
though the ladies prefer smaller designs, discreetly placed;
little pictures such as an apple with a bite taken out, or a
dainty Bambi. Ages range from 18-year-olds (tattooing
anyone below the age of 18 is illegal) to pensioners; most are
in their mid-20s and with the current popularity of tattoos,
some days most of the customers may be women.

Tattoo artists' shops have walls and models adorned with a

choice of patterns, plus catalogues filled with more designs. Work is done using a transfer, or freehand. Each design is priced: a simple one that takes half an hour costs around £35, whereas a large work involving up to three sittings is priced at about £40 to £50 per hour. Although tattooing is quite painful, it is 'bearable' and some customers may have a two-hour session, while for others ten minutes is enough. Average time for a session is 30 minutes.

Hands, faces and necks are not touched by the professional tattoo artists, because customers may regret their hastiness later. As they are walking advertisements, it is the summer time, when shirts and tee-shirts come off, that is the busiest season for the tattooists. Much admired, then, are colourful designs such as glorious birds of paradise; cartoons, perhaps with as many as ten characters, attract interest, too. So you'll be very busy in July and August – and catch up with your reading in January and February.

A tattoo artist's equipment costs around £2000 to £5000 and includes an electric machine, inks bought in powder pigment form and mixed before use with antiseptic, and disposable needles. There is special emphasis on hygiene. Under a 1982 Act, designed then to prevent the spread of hepatitis B, now essential to reassure customers about AIDS prevention, tattoo artists must be registered and licensed by the local health authority. Ear piercing, acupuncture and electrolysis are covered by the same legislation. All inks and needles are thrown away after use, as they are in a hospital.

Equipment is obtained through APTA – but you need to be already working as a tattooist to qualify for it, so you need to be determined about getting started.

Training is normally done by working with an experienced tattoo artist, though many are self-taught. Some of the first jobs may consist of improving the shoddy work of the back street (illegal) cowboys and the skills are gradually developed with experience.

Theatrical Wigmaker

CONTACT: Theatrical wigmakers (London); opera companies;
             theatres; BBC

SALARY: From £80 per day, freelance

SKILLS: Patience; good eyesight; concentration

Department of almost useless information: the hair used for wigmaking is natural 'virgin' hair, not cut but saved from the brushes of women and girls in the villages of southern Italy, who have never had their long tresses permed, bleached or coloured; or bought as cut hair from girls in Greece. It is then sent to be sorted strand by strand, and boiled and cleaned until it is sterilised, then gathered into bundles, all in different colours.

The wigs themselves are seen on the West End stage, videos and TV commercials, theatres and opera houses around the country. The effect may be of the weird and wonderful variety, such as a flamboyant pantomime wig, or an attention-catching design for a TV commercial. Or they may reflect an historical period – not only of the first Elizabethan age, but also the forties, with the hair swept up at the back and pinned into place with grips and (modern) hairspray. Wigs made of natural European hair are valuable – one that reached to the floor was worth £1000.

A theatrical production has a designer who works on the show with a hairdresser who specifies what type of wigs are needed for the characters. Then the actresses visit the wigmaker to have their fittings and for colours to be sorted out. Either a new wig may be made up from scratch, or a wig from stock will be altered and dyed to match the specification. Wigs are normally hired for use during a production and returned afterwards. Not only top-of-the-head hair, of course – beards and moustaches may be false, too.

Wigmaking is divided into four processes. First there is the foundation, a lace base of tiny squares. Then comes the knotting; hair is knotted on to the foundation in the same way that a rug is made. Round the hairline only one hair is knotted each time, so that the effect looks very real; over the rest of the head, four hairs are knotted together, in different directions to make the hair move in a certain way, and give the effect of a parting. When the wig knotter has put the hair on to the base, it is permanently dyed and treated, and finally the wig dresser styles and cuts it. The whole process is done by hand, and normally takes several weeks.

School leavers may be taken on by wigmakers (although there are not many openings) and trained on the job. Courses in theatre wardrobe include wigmaking, such as those at the London College of Fashion and Wimbledon School of Art. Two-year full-time courses in hairdressing and beauty at further education colleges can include basic knotting for wigmaking, and give the chance to finish as a stylist. It usually takes about six months to learn all the techniques of knotting to get a natural look, and a year to master them completely. Knotting is a slow process demanding concentration on a very small area; those who feel they must be able to look around them sometimes, have more chance to exercise creative flair, and work under pressure to meet deadlines, may prefer being a wig dresser.

Apart from the wigmakers in London, the BBC and large theatres such as the Coliseum have their own wig dressers; outside London, opera companies such as Glyndebourne and Opera North, and the theatre at Stratford also have their own. Salaries are not high; the best chances are in work for TV advertisements, and in theatres where it is possible to work overtime.

A wigmaker can work as a freelance, alternating between work for theatre companies, films (where a close-up 18 feet wide means everything has to look perfect!) or on mock-ups for photographs to illustrate a book on fashions in Ancient Egypt. A top freelance can earn £144 a day.

So the next time you visit the theatre, perhaps you will be wondering: are those natural-looking long locks really hers – or a cover-up for her own cropped hair?

Tree Surgeon

CONTACT: Arboricultural Association, Ampfield House,
Ampfield, Nr Romsey, Hampshire SO51 9PA;
01794 368717

EARNINGS: Around £350 per week

SKILLS: Interest in trees; no fear of heights

Dangling from a rope at the top of a tall tree is an unnerving experience – it seems as though there is nothing at all underneath. It is not like standing at the top of a tall building or cliff, where there is at least solid ground underfoot. Climbing to the top of the tree would be very pleasant for most surgeons – but in this occupation it can be a risky way to make a living.

The tools are different, too: not a scalpel but a chainsaw. However, the principles are the same – of cutting out diseased parts, trying to save when possible and caring about health and nutrition.

Tree surgeons are concerned with amenity trees in parks and gardens, working for private customers, or for a local authority. Unlike foresters, who deal with whole forests or stretches of woodland using fast-moving machinery, the tree surgeons deal with single trees. They cope with broken branches, or branches that are too close to a power line, and taking down diseased trees, or those that are growing too close to a public road. The equipment they use is basically simple: ropes, a chainsaw and climbing harnesses.

Many 'loppers and toppers' have learnt their skills through experience, but there are nine colleges in differing parts of the country offering various training courses. Longest established is Merrist Wood Agricultural College, Worplesdon, Guildford, Surrey, where there are short courses in chainsaw use and maintenance and a safety training course in tree climbing. The college also offers more advanced courses, including a ten-week course for craftsmen which starts in

September and covers tree biology, identifying features of trees, soil types, pests and diseases and other tree problems, trees and the law, and tree work machinery; it leads to a College Certificate. There is also a one-year National Certificate course in Horticulture (Arboriculture) and a three-year National Diploma course in Arboriculture. Grants for the courses may be available from the local authority, or a local firm specialising in tree surgery will give on-the-job training and may be prepared to send a trainee to college. Many tree surgery firms shut down during the summer, and recruit only from November to the end of February.

Tripe Dresser

CONTACT: National Association of Tripe Dressers,
60 Claremont Road, Surbiton, Surrey KT6 4RH;
0181 390 2022

SALARY: Average, £250 per week

SKILLS: Willingness to work in steaming, wet conditions

If you have ever been in Spain and chosen *callos* on the restaurant menu, then you have eaten tripe, probably cooked in a sauce of tomatoes, wine, spices and bacon. It is a very popular food in Spain, and in France, too. In this country footballers used to eat it before a match because it is easily digestible, but the recipe is usually of the boring old tripe-onions-and-milk variety. More exciting, ready-cooked and vacuum-packed tripe dishes are to be found in Continental delicatessens, supplied by enterprising tripe-dressing firms keen to increase demand.

Strictly speaking, tripe dressing is one part of the cleaning routine. Tripe is cow's stomach; cows are liberally supplied with stomachs, having four in all, and the tripe may be black on arrival, if the animal has been grazing on the coal-rich ground of Wales. The end product, sold in the shops, is creamy white (the second stomach is called 'Bible' tripe because it has so many paper-like leaves; 'honeycomb' tripe comes from the main stomach). In between is washing by machine and lots of hot water, dressing (peeling off the outer skin), cooking and bleaching with a whitening agent – each tripe dresser has a secret whitening recipe. The product is then either made up into continental-style meals or despatched to the butchers' and supermarkets where it is sold for eating 'raw' in summer with mayonnaise or vinegar, or cooked in a hot casserole in winter.

Tripe dressers have been around for centuries; some of the recipes for tripe came over from France with the Conqueror. It is more popular now in its northern strongholds of Lancashire and Yorkshire, where most of the firms are. Cheap to buy (about £1.08 per lb retail), nutritious and low in fat, and cooked in a French- or Spanish-style savoury sauce, or marinated and then fried in breadcrumbs, it could be set for new gastronomic success – properly dressed, of course.

Typesetter

CONTACT: Typesetting firms (Yellow Pages); British Printing
            Industries Federation, 11 Bedford Row, London
            WC1R 4DX; 0171 242 6904

SALARY: £363.80 (average) per week

SKILLS: Typing skills; manual dexterity; good English
            language qualifications; not colour blind

The changes in typesetting have been revolutionary in recent years: instead of making up lines of type using back-to-front alphabet characters and numbers made of lead metal, the text goes on to a floppy disk through the keyboard of a computer and the work can be seen and checked on a VDU screen. The result is, of course, that all-male bastions have fallen to the flying fingers of women, who may have changed jobs from former lives as copy-typists or telex operators. The GPMU (Graphical, Paper and Media Union) has several thousand 'lady' keyboarding members, and there are several 'mixed' firms. There are also some where the typesetters are all girls.

Girls who enter a firm as skilled touch-typists then have to learn about setting up the computer, loading the work on to it and setting it out into columns and blocks. There are the mysteries of typesetting to be assimilated, such as type-faces, point sizes, ems (in which column widths are measured), line spacing and tabular work. Training is on the job and can take three months, depending on aptitude.

Men used to be trained by apprenticeships lasting around six years; now the training period for a school leaver is much shorter. Traineeships with the British Printing Industries Federation scheme last from two years and combine on-the-job training with City and Guilds qualifications. Different companies use different computer systems with the result that typesetters who have worked on newspapers have to re-train with a new system, such as Scantext, for other work. The computers themselves have as many as 2000 possible type-faces to choose from; but only a small proportion are used regularly.

While work for some printers may be dull, such as government work that includes all those Green and White Papers or figure and tabular work, other typesetters work for companies that set up the type for books, magazines, local or special interest newspapers or advertising agencies (who still sometimes use metal type). The less boring the work, and the more fascinating the reading, the fewer mistakes.

Copy that arrives to be typeset varies from handwritten 'squiggly doctor's writing' that needs good eyesight, to typewritten pages. The typesetter selects the type-faces on the computer for headings or main copy, and fixes column widths or box sizes, and keys it in. When the copy has been typeset it goes back to the customer as galleys or page proofs for corrections to be made, and those corrections then have to be transferred on to the computer.

Often the layout designers will ask for the copy to be set to an awkward shape to fit round a sketch or illustration. Designers and paste-up artists may work together in, occasionally, a madhouse atmosphere, with ten jobs being done at once, and deadlines to be met. Once the typesetting and corrections have been completed, the work is normally sent to another firm (often in another country) to be printed.

There are still a few printers around the country using metal type, which can be quicker when the work is of the letterheadings or business card variety, but this is a dying trade. With computers speeding up the work there are not so many jobs around, and there is still the tradition in some firms that jobs go to relations of staff. In firms where there is a closed shop there is little chance to do overtime. Rates in non-union houses (mainly outside London) are lower, but with more overtime worked; staff may work regular extra shifts up to as late as midnight three days a week on a six-day week.

There can be high rewards for typesetters who set up in the right place, aim for the right market, and can attract enough customers. A new system plus word-processor can cost around £20,000, whereas old, non-digital equipment may cost as little as £12,000.

Yacht Crewmember

CONTACT: Get to know the right people through joining a yacht club and visiting marinas, in the UK or Mediterranean, and the right 'yachtie' pubs!

EARNINGS: From £20 per day

SKILLS: Sailing experience

A job delivering yachts to the Caribbean, Canada, the States, even Guadaloupe, or scrubbing the decks and manning the wheel on a millionaire's St Tropez-based gin palace really does not sound too mundane a way of life.

Agencies who run charter yachts in the Mediterranean, or offer their services to owners who want their boats moved from one part of the world to another, receive a steady stream of letters from would-be crewmembers. In the case of the charter yachts, the boats are privately owned and available for charter, and the owners appoint their own crew on board, normally by recommendation; people move easily from boat to boat in the South of France. Some crew are taken on for nothing, as a summer season holiday experience, but rates for permanent crew would vary from £630 per month (with no experience) for deckhands and stewardesses, to over £3800 per month, with highest salaries for the captain, berth mate and (*cordon bleu*) cook. Deck hands and stewardesses are also usually well experienced on the charter yachts, earning up to £1900 per month.

If a boat is chartered it could mean three months of sailing around the South of France, Turkey, Greece and Italy; but if there is no charter there is three months of sitting alongside the quay. The much larger boats, up to 250ft, are not always available for charter, so the crew is only at sea when the owner is on board – which may be every week, or only two or three days a year.

Holiday companies that run cruising yacht flotillas around the coasts of Greece, Turkey and Yugoslavia take on skippers to run the flotillas, diesel mechanics and hostesses. Skippers and mechanics work from March to November, with the initial two months spent preparing the boats ashore. Hostesses do not necessarily need sailing experience, but it is an advantage, along with common sense, initiative and languages.

Owners of boats worth perhaps £150,000 who want them delivered from maybe Athens to Vancouver, and the insurance companies who take them on, expect the skipper who takes charge of them to be a highly experienced sailor, and to have the Yachtmaster certificates of the RYA and Department of Trade and Industry. The skipper recruits the crew, who may be paid £20 per day all found (food and return flight). Some may be virtually beginners, taken on for short trips, and given tuition with no pay except food and expenses. For longer trips the skipper will expect experience and knowledge of navigation and he may take new applicants across the busy shipping lanes of the Channel to evaluate their capabilities. A skipper would charge around £75 per day; an engineer, £50.

Once they have been accepted on to the crew list, crewmembers let the skipper know when they are likely to be available for delivery trips. Courses for Yachtmaster certificates, for whose who are thinking of becoming more than casual crewmembers, are organised by sailing schools ashore; other courses include Competent Crew, Day Skipper and Coastal Skipper. Rather more advanced is the fully commercial ticket qualification needed for the skippers of the high-tonnage super cruisers of the Mediterranean, who live permanently on board with their families and can be salaried at £30,000 to £45,500 pa.

A word of warning: though walking the jetties in spring looking for a berth is a romantic way of finding a job, it is important to ask for references and check that the people you are sailing with are reputable. The smuggling (and planting) of drugs is a fact of life, which is why Customs and Excise 'rummage' crews give a thorough going-over to incoming boats, and there are pirates operating in the Caribbean, even in the twentieth century.

Also from Kogan Page

Second edition

Test Your Own Aptitude

Jim Barrett and Geoff Williams

Working on their belief that people who know their own strengths have a far better chance of being successful, the authors provide a series of scientifically determined tests and questionnaires which enable readers to evaluate their own aptitude. The results can then be matched to the requirements of over 400 job titles listed in the book.

Paperback ISBN 1-85091-919-4

A full list of careers and vocational titles is available from Kogan Page, 120 Pentonville Road, London N1 9JN; telephone 0171-278 0433.